DEALSTORMING

DEALSTORMING

The Secret Weapon That Can Solve

Your Toughest Sales Challenges

TIM SANDERS

PORTFOLIO / PENGUIN

PORTFOLIO / PENGUIN
An imprint of Penguin Random House LLC
375 Hudson Street
New York, New York 10014
penguin.com

Illustrations by Anthony Cuccia

Library of Congress Cataloging-in-Publication Data

Names: Sanders, Tim, 1961– author.
Title: Dealstorming : the secret weapon that can solve your toughest sales
challenges / Tim Sanders.
Description: New York, New York : Portfolio, 2016.
Identifiers: LCCN 2015044501 (print) | LCCN 2015050023 (ebook) |
ISBN 9781591848219 (hardback) | ISBN 9780698408210 (ebook)
Subjects: LCSH: Sales management. | Decision making. | Teams in the workplace. |
BISAC: BUSINESS & ECONOMICS / Sales & Selling. | BUSINESS & ECONOMICS /
Decision Making & Problem Solving.
Classification: LCC HF5438.4 .S2654 2016 (print) | LCC HF5438.4 (ebook) |
DDC 658.8/1—dc23
LC record available at http://lccn.loc.gov/2015044501

Printed in the United States of America
3 5 7 9 10 8 6 4 2

To my wife, Jacqueline,
who fills my life with blue skies
and sunny days.

Contents

DEALSTORMING

Introduction: Don't Go Down Alone

I t was a cold, overcast day in the fall of 1997. Stan Woodward, our new vice president of business services at Audionet (which would later become Broadcast.com), was leading his first team meeting in our makeshift conference area. We huddled around him with keen interest, wondering what he was going to tell us. After all, he was a seasoned sales leader from the technology industry, brought in by our founders, Mark Cuban and Todd Wagner, to take our revenue production "to the next level."

Stan spoke slowly as his right hand rubbed coins together in his pocket. "When you see an opportunity for us to bill a lot of money and produce a happy customer, don't walk away from it if you get stuck," he said. "Don't go down alone! Don't. Go down. Alone!"

Stan came from a world of multimillion-dollar deals at startups like Fibermux and Ascend, where each sale was the difference between living to fight another day and folding. "You can't give up on the good ones," he told us. "When you're stuck, look for help. Even people who don't commission on the deal are here to help you, especially those who will deliver your promises. Don't just rely on your sales manager for all the solutions. Go wide if you have to." He repeated, "Don't go down alone. Gather a team, put your brains together, and make it rain!"

At that moment, two concepts collided in the front of my mind. To solve the tough, must-win sale, Stan was telling us to combine two distinct practices that had long been thought of as separate arenas, especially in sales: *deal making* and *brainstorming.* The former was a linear process requiring discipline; the latter was a freewheeling process that promoted lateral thinking. I thought, *He's right. If we put these two approaches together, we can crack some tough cases.* I remember leaning over and whispering to my coworker: "Cool beans. *Dealstorming!*"

Previously in my career, solving sales challenges meant opening a discussion with my manager, in which he reviewed my steps to make sure I'd crossed every *t* and dotted every *i*. Often it led to the directive to either make one more attempt to close, offer better terms, or give up and move on because "they aren't serious buyers."

Stan's point was that we should take advantage of the collective intelligence of our coworkers to figure out how to get the must-do deal done. He recognized that big opportunities were scarce, and sometimes best practices and following a strict, no-deviation process weren't good enough. Because Audionet was a startup with an IPO in its near future, he knew that we'd have no problem convincing nonsales employees to come to our aid.

I took his lead and began organizing what I coined "dealstorms" to tackle high-difficulty sales opportunities. Leaning on my previous experience working in the personnel development department at Hughes Aircraft, where I facilitated cross-departmental meetings to improve quality at the plant, I designed a multidisciplinary approach to problem solving. I recruited fellow employees who either knew something about the prospect company or would be responsible for coding, programming, or participating in the broadcast if we won the deal. At first, I followed traditional brainstorming rules for the meetings (go for a lot of ideas, build on each other's ideas) and then applied standard deal-making principles for follow-up (define value, drive agreement).

Over the next year, dealstorm breakthroughs led to webcasting deals with Harvard University, management guru Tom Peters, and Victoria's Secret. But in several cases, according to Stan Woodward, our dealstorming meetings were more like "goat rodeos" than structured problem-solving sessions. He accurately pointed out that a few of the key principles of brainstorming (wild ideas are encouraged, debate is discouraged) don't work well in business-to-business sales situations. Also, not all participants understood clearly their roles in the process we had designed.

With his astute critiques in mind, I set out to define a repeatable, sales-centric process that respected everyone's time as well as produced progress with every meeting. I pored over research and compared notes with my customers and acquaintances at Intel, Cisco, and PBS's The Business Channel. With each dealstorm, I tweaked my approach and then followed up with participants to get their feedback.

Based on these insights, I arrived at my new and improved definition of dealstorming: to organize and lead a cross-functional team to work together to solve a significant sales challenge through highly structured meetings and project work.

A few years later, after Yahoo! acquired Broadcast.com, I was transferred to headquarters to support the chief sales officer, Anil Singh. The dot-com crash was upon us, and we needed to replace dead startup clients with big brands—and quickly. Landing deals with Fortune 500 companies was our ticket to survival.

I was given license to network with account executives and sales managers across Yahoo! to find situations where I could apply my dealstorming technique to help them win extreme-difficulty deals or renew accounts at risk. After a few high-profile successes, Anil approved resources for me to create a team to scale my efforts. I named our group the ValueLab and recruited a few researchers straight out of graduate school, along with a former Cisco analyst. Our charter was to serve as the idea machine for key accounts, with a focus on demonstrating the value of Yahoo!'s assets to prospects and existing customers.

Knowing that I'd need to step up my game, I continued to research all things collaboration, including brainstorming facilitation, creative problem solving, innovation, and project management. I realized that we needed to improve the preparation we conducted prior to meetings, so we added a new step to dealstorming: the parse. This was a three- to four-page brief that succinctly outlined the sales challenge, efforts to date, the players involved, and background on the prospect company and its market. The ValueLab worked closely with account executives, our marketing research group, and sales operations to make each parse a discussion driver that produced results faster than could be achieved by simply throwing people into a room.

One of our first projects took us to Burbank to work on the Disney Studios account and grow our movie-marketing business. At the time, Disney marketing executives didn't see online media as an effective way to put millions of butts in seats on opening weekend. They liked the volume of impressions that network television spots and newspaper display ads could deliver.

The account executive and I recruited a wide dealstorming team to solve the Disney Studios problem. We invited every Yahoo! employee who could potentially touch the Disney account, not just in sales but in engineering, marketing, design, and data mining. We also invited anyone with expertise in the movie industry or product launch promotions to participate in the dealstorm. We knew that input from multiple departments would be required to drive any significant relationship with the studio.

Although ideas came from individuals, solutions emerged as the result of the group's collaborative efforts to improve them into a workable plan. We were harnessing group intelligence to create unexpected but effective plans. As it turned out, sales genius didn't come solely from individual sales reps, my researchers, or me. Sales genius, I discovered, is a team sport. It was about all of us in the room finding and solving problems as one.

The Disney experience also verified that questioning our assumptions was a pivotal part of the process, as important as coming up with solution ideas. Everyone on the team was encouraged to ask questions about our assumed problem. Are we pitching the wrong products or services? Are we selling to the right people? Is there a higher-order problem or opportunity that we should be discussing?

These questions led to breakthroughs (and a few heated debates). For example, in one of our first Disney dealstorming meetings, one of our data-mining engineers asked, "Are we leading with our strongest value-add to their overall marketing plan? Can our search data give us a pretty good idea of how well their television advertising is working? Couldn't we look at search activity after the Sunday newspaper ads come out, to see if it's really lifting interest?" In other words, do we really need to focus on selling media impressions, or should we position ourselves as a vital part of an efficient movie launch plan?

That created a paradigm shift in our thinking because our assumption all along was that our sales strategy was to help Disney generate awareness of a new movie, which meant that we focused on pitching promotional ideas and media only. But the fact remained that Disney could reach more people by buying an ad on the network sitcom *Friends* than by placing a banner ad on our home page for an entire day. We realized that the winning value proposition could be providing Disney with insights about the millions of dollars it was already spending on television and newspaper advertising for each release and then augmenting its approach with our media and promotions.

One of our marketing managers suggested that we go further than postcampaign analysis and see whether we could help Disney with campaign planning. A data-mining engineer on the team concocted an algorithm using our search data to measure how much interest Disney's traditional advertising was generating. The data was so rich that we were able to predict with stunning accuracy opening weekend box office revenue several days in advance.

This change in our value proposition kicked the door wide open for us at Disney because the studio president was very focused on optimizing their promotional ad programs. Once he and his team put the pencil to the potential cost savings our insights could provide, they moved forward with a several-hundred-thousand-dollar program. Once inside the account, we convinced the Disney marketing team to test and scale various online promotions, leading to a multimillion-dollar deal. This is the power of questioning assumptions prior to launching into idea-making mode.

Over the course of the next few years, the ValueLab participated in over fifty dealstorms with advertising and business services account executives. After I left Yahoo!, I continued to teach and run dealstorms as a consultant for clients in industries ranging from technology services to defense contractors to business process outsourcing to marketing solutions providers. This is when I developed my train-the-client approach, helping each one become self-sufficient at creating and leading dealstorms after a few projects, allowing them to scale this new way of problem solving across the company.

To write this book, I interviewed over two hundred sales leaders from around the world—including chief revenue officers, sales vice presidents, directors, and process-oriented account executives—to compare notes and discover how they've used elements of dealstorming to tackle sales issues of all types. In many cases, I found useful tools to add to my process as well as examples of where creative collaboration led to breakthrough performance. Over and over again, I confirmed that to be truly competitive in today's selling environment, every sales organization needs to implement a repeatable process to quickly problem solve their greatest challenges.

Dealstorming is a problem-solving technique I've developed over the last fifteen years into a repeatable, cyclical process that has evolved to include the following seven steps: qualify, organize, prepare, convene, execute, analyze, and report. This book will go much deeper into each of these steps, but in general, here's what each one does:

- ➤ **Qualify:** Sales managers assess the need for collaboration and then calculate the resources required for a dealstorm based on the significance of the challenge as well as its level of difficulty or the inability of the current sales process to solve it.

- ➤ **Organize:** Account executives organize the dealstorming team based on who knows something about the problem space or will be affected by the outcome.

- ➤ **Prepare:** Account executives prepare their teams by writing a comprehensive but compact deal brief that frames the challenge and gives everyone involved key information related to the sales challenge.

- ➤ **Convene:** The team convenes for a dealstorming meeting that is tightly facilitated and utilizes templates and exercises for problem and solution finding.

- ➤ **Execute:** The account executive is responsible for managing execution of ideas from the meeting, with the help of team members.

- ➤ **Analyze:** After implementation, efforts should be analyzed by the account executive and sales manager to see whether they worked and whether new problems have been identified, requiring more dealstorming meetings.

➤ **Report:** Dealstorm progress should be reported to each team member, along with notifications about future meetings (if required). If the dealstorm was successful, any innovations should be shared with sales leadership to improve the system going forward.

In the event the deal is still stuck after the seven steps have been completed, the account executive will need to reconvene the team to discuss the problems that remain and explore new strategies. In that case, there will be a new round of analysis and reporting. This cycle continues until the sales challenge is solved, the account executive has gained sufficient insights to proceed alone, or the sales manager deems the opportunity unwinnable.

Each step is critical to the success of the process. Too often, people focus only on the convene (meeting) step, thinking that's all a dealstorm requires. This stems from long-standing corporate use of the brainstorming technique, a one-off exercise in which a group of people are assembled and then led on an extemporaneous search for new ideas without any preparation, vetting, or execution process in place. While it's handy for creating a quick list of ideas, the complexity of today's sales challenges requires much more work before, during, and after team meetings.

While the emphasis of the book is on this process, I'll also share perspectives with you regarding sales methodology, leadership, innovation, and creativity that will be helpful in leading sales organizations, implementing dealstorms, or participating in them. And though much of the advice is written specifically for sales leaders and account executives, all members of the sales organization, as well as groups that support them, should be well versed in how the process works and how each one can be a valuable resource to the dealstorming team.

This book is intended to complement your existing sales methodology, be it the Miller Heiman Strategic Selling approach, Solution Selling, the Challenger Sale concept, Diagnostic Business Development, SPIN Selling, or the Sandler Selling System. With each of those methodologies, useful as they are, there will be times when a prospective sale gets stuck or an existing relationship is endangered. That's where dealstorming can be used as a tool to get the process back on track.

This book is organized into three parts: "The Case for Sales Collaboration," "The Dealstorming Method," and "Tools for Innovation." In "The Case for Sales Collaboration," the first chapter outlines the increasing complexity of today's business-to-business (B2B) sales. I'll document how prospects and customers are organizing into buying teams, especially for larger expenditures. Chapter 2 will introduce the idea that a done deal is a host of problems solved, not the result of a single big idea or stellar pitch. I'll reveal the four levels of each sale: contact, conceive, convince, and contract. Chapter 3 will explain how solving a sales challenge requires wide teams that consciously collaborate in a highly structured and well-managed process.

"The Dealstorming Method" is divided into four chapters that outline the dealstorming cycle in detail. Chapter 4 introduces *qualify* and *organize*—how to properly staff and equip a dealstorm, whom to recruit, and how to persuade them to join the team. Chapter 5 focuses on *prepare*—the importance of premeeting preparation and how to construct a deal brief to guide the team. Chapter 6 details *convene*—how to set up and then facilitate meetings so that they are productive and lead to collaborative breakthroughs. Chapter 7 covers *execute, analyze,* and *report*—what needs to be done after meetings, including verifying claims and assumptions, executing plans, analyzing progress, and reporting to the team and management.

"Tools for Success" goes beyond the nuts and bolts of the process and offers additional ways to drive problem solving. Chapter 8 introduces three personas that any member of a dealstorm can take on to unleash innovative thinking. Chapter 9 expands the notion of dealstorming beyond the internal team to include external champions and mentors. Chapter 10 documents the connection between strong relationships and creative performance. It argues that to lead a sales team or a dealstorm, you need to expand your circle of high-quality relationships through valued exchanges.

The dealstorming process combined with these innovative tools and perspectives is like a Swiss Army knife for today's toughest sales challenges—useful in a variety of situations. And with each dealstorm, you'll gain more insights on how and when to use the process to compress the sales cycle or increase renewals rates. You'll improve your ability to lead project groups and deepen relationships with them as well.

This book will give you a powerful tool for managing your pipeline of sales opportunities and preserving key account relationships. Between my Yahoo! and consulting experience, dealstorming solved the big sales problem an organization faced—be it closing a deal, renewing one, or restoring a broken relationship—over 70% of the time. For new account opportunities, dealstorms compressed the typical or predicted sales cycle by 25%.

The reason dealstorming is so powerful is because it greatly improves the quality of information and the depth of options available to solve the sales challenge. When you have more relevant insights, you possess the raw materials required for innovation. In many cases, the team codeveloped winning strategies during the sessions. This has the additional benefit of improving postsale delivery, especially when everyone who touches the account is involved from the start. It also improves solidarity between sales, operations, and other parts of the company. No longer will other departments feel like work is being "thrown over the wall," but instead that such work is jointly defined and agreed upon.

Dealstorming can strengthen the collaborative fabric of your sales organization and, by extension, your entire company. Culture is a conversation, led by leaders, about "how we do things effectively here." When a group's culture is strong, there is a collective intuition about what each person on the team should do in a given situation. When we promote cross-discipline collaboration through launching dealstorms, it becomes a natural response to sales and business problems over time. Stan Woodward encouraged us to team up when faced with a worthy challenge; you need to do the same with your account executives or colleagues. "One team, one company" needs to become a consistent part of the conversation at work. With this book, you'll have a process to walk the talk.

As you'll soon discover, the best sales-driven companies in the world have developed the habit of conscious collaboration across departments and disciplines. They've developed the perspective that no boundaries should limit their ability to land the plum account or keep key client relationships going strong. They embody the Navy SEAL mantra that "individuals play the game, but teams beat the odds."

THE CASE FOR SALES COLLABORATION

CHAPTER I

It's Getting Tougher Out There

I n 1976, my friends and I hung out regularly at the Laundromat on Main Street, sinking quarters into our thrilling new pastime: *Pong.* *Pong* was a two-dimensional arcade game experience that mimicked the table tennis we played on my back porch.

Unlike playing card or board games, winning at *Pong* required hand–eye coordination to keep a bleeping bar of a ball in play. Though it was a simple game, it was addictive—at least until you mastered it, which could be done in a few long weekends, especially if you bought a gaming console and played at home for free.

A few years later, I graduated to more sophisticated games, like *Asteroids, Space Invaders,* and *Donkey Kong.* These games were more complex: more obstacles, more hazards, and, most important, more levels. For gamers, the excitement and the accomplishment was all about breaking through increasingly difficult levels in pursuit of the high score.

When I went off to college in the '80s, I discovered *Ultima,* an immersive, fantasy role-playing computer gaming experience where wizards and demons challenged me as I attempted to ascend multiple levels. Hand–eye coordination still mattered in battle or for navigating mazelike rooms, but problem-solving skills were required for success, to actually level up. This was quickly followed by increasingly complex offerings, including shoot-'em-up game *Doom* and world simulation game *Civilization*.

Fast-forward to today: games like *Halo* and *World of Warcraft* present dizzying challenges to even the most skilled players in the world. Levels are counted in the hundreds instead of the dozens. Narrative overlays make story solving as much of the game as hunting, defending, or unlocking clues while multiplayer environments make it almost impossible for a mere mortal to ever actually finish the game.

Winning one of these video games is significantly harder than it was in the *Pong* days—and it's getting tougher every day. So is closing a deal in the fast-moving, highly complicated world of B2B sales.

For as long as I can remember, I've been a salesperson. I ran a fireworks stand during the summer as a young teen and in high school; in the late 1970s, I repped a radio station in eastern New Mexico. Station KKQQ-FM played progressive rock and Top 40, and it was there where I learned the art of "selling air." This was my foray into the world of B2B sales.

The station manager assigned me the nearby township of Portales as my territory and, over a long lunch, trained me in the basics of selling. His key points were: It's a numbers game. Stick with the script. Always be closing.

With rate card in hand, wearing a new white shirt and clip-on tie, I hit the bricks.

It was a simple time for a radio salesperson. I went door to door, visiting retail business owners to see if they would like to increase their foot traffic through a radio promotion. If they'd done it before and it worked, it was my lucky day. If they'd tried a campaign or two and it didn't work, I had a mountain to climb to get them to buy again. If they'd never tried radio ads before, I had to convince them it was worth their money by sharing relevant success stories.

Closing the deal was simple: Get the order signed and pick up the check. No contract or back-and-forth negotiations. Deal or no deal.

If the radio ads worked and my customers saw a bump in their business, I earned a renewal. If they didn't, well, I either moved on or tried to convince them to take a new tack the next time.

To my manager's credit, his advice was mostly useful. It *was* a numbers game, and "loading the funnel" was the secret to success. For anyone who sold just about anything during those days, it was likely just as simple: one product, one or two decision makers, and very little confounding technology or paperwork to deal with.

A decade or so later, I graduated to selling television advertising and, later, digital marketing and enterprise technology solutions. As the years went on, selling became more complicated. Instead of selling to an owner or a single decision maker, I had to persuade buying committees or multiple departmental heads. No longer did I sell a single product or service; the customer wanted an entire solution, with a suite of options. Instead of demonstrating product benefits to prospects, I had to calculate their total cost of buying and managing my solutions (aka total cost of ownership). Simple purchase agreements were replaced by lengthy contracts.

Sure, there are still the straightforward sales situations, such as a print shop clerk replenishing business cards for a local shop or an electronics store employee selling a computer monitor to a customer, just like you can still play solitaire. But you don't build a great business with transactional sales. You must build game-changing solutions and then help them find a market by navigating complexity throughout the sales process.

Gone are the days of playing the numbers game and winning. Sure, even "back in the day" you had a handful of tough sales, usually because of difficult prospects or bureaucratic companies; but in the end, if you worked the system, the system worked for you. Today, tough sales are the norm. Creating a new enterprise account is just as challenging as climbing to the top level of *Halo*.

Sales complexity, the addition of steps and variables, is rising as a result of four developments: more decision makers and influencers, more information at our prospect's fingertips, increasingly complex technology in our products and services, and more competitors to battle in the marketplace. This is why you need a sophisticated process like dealstorming to cut through the clutter of obstacles that stand in your way.

First, for those selling business solutions, the sale is no longer made belly to belly, where a demo and a strong pitch leads to a nodding head and a signed contract. There are many more moving parts involved—more steps, more stuff. That's the reality of today's selling landscape. Today's B2B sales professional must navigate a rising tide of decision makers, influencers, cosigners, and stakeholders. With each new person who is introduced to the selling situation, new perspectives and individual needs must be accounted for, making the sale even tougher.

In the world of technology- and software-based solutions, the number of influencers in the purchase decision is expanding rapidly. Applications sales manager Dan Craig and his team rep an Oracle software solution (CX) that organizes the customer experience around all touch points. His is a relatively new business unit. "Being with Oracle, you'd think the sale is made in IT," Dan told me. "But that's just the entry point where they vet that it works with their systems or warrants a 'rip and replace.' To win, you need to get to the business leads who care about its benefits, such as the VP of marketing or VP of sales. That's a radically different conversation, where you quickly need to learn their language and then discover their unique pain points."

The shift from selling to IT to selling to all these other point people at the prospect organization is a radical departure for B2B sales teams. According to Dan, "it's like the difference between speaking Greek and talking basketball technique."

His experience is not uncommon. Research firm International Data Corporation (IDC) conducted a buyer survey that revealed that the number of decision makers for a technology sale was rising at a rate of almost 15% year over year.[1] With the involvement of technology, business, operations, and finance leads, the field is turning into a consortium of buyers who all must be convinced. And this explosion of new selling targets isn't unique to the tech space. The Corporate Executive Board calculates that there are over five decision makers involved in the average enterprise sale, across all categories. In the opinion of some of the sales leaders I've surveyed, this estimate might be coming in on the low side.

Consider the training and development solutions space, where today's instructors employ digital media and software instead of yesteryear's videotapes, three-ring binders, and printed self-assessments. You might think that the sales rep's job is to get to the training and development director and maybe the human resources executive who approves bigger budget allocations at one of these companies. But that's not the case. At Skillsoft, a corporate learning and talent management provider, an enterprise deal involves many decision makers and a slew of influencers. While the learning and development director in HR plays quarterback, her manager-clients, IT engineers, finance analysts, and field trainers all weigh in on the final decision.

Your team doesn't sell to a few people anymore. Today, they lobby to a committee.

It's not just the extra personalities, either. The theater of sales has changed as well. "It's not like my experience years ago at Xerox, where you walked into a face-to-face meeting with the decision maker or key executives," said Skillsoft executive Tom Cunningham. "Today, they are spread out all over the world, working virtually on global initiatives that somehow touch your sale. The days of an individual signing in front of us are o-v-e-r."

A few decades ago, when technology and telecommunications

products started to gobble up big chunks of corporate budgets, the information technology (IT) department was created to play gate-keeper and supervisor. With their expertise, the IT department could cut through the tech jargon and vet proposed equipment and services for their true efficacy.

Over the years, more influencers and decisions makers were added to the deal-making process, including finance department analysts, operations managers, end users of the products, and in-house buying specialists. In some cases, you'll have to square off against your prospect's sales leaders, brought into the process to provide insight into your selling tactics. We see increasing sophistication on the part of the buyer, as the hierarchy has been decentralized into areas of excellence specializing in all aspects of a purchase, from money to technology to business development to operations.

Today, when sales systems are a science and dollars are stretched thin from one economic recovery to the next bubble burst, there's an additional layer of scrutiny that sales leaders and account executives have to punch through: the procurement department. When there's a big check to be written, procurement committees or vendor boards get involved. Sales process experts such as Jeffrey Thull believe that this development is a response to increasingly aggressive sales tactics employed against harried buyers.[2] Even though their presence slows down the buying process for managers who might need the solution in place quickly, the risk of getting burned frightens the company and outweighs the hassle factor of clearing procurement.

And while in-house procurement groups are tough to bring to consensus, they don't hold a candle to the cost-cutting ruthlessness of procurement consultants, such as GEP or Bain. B2B buyer surveys reveal that there has been a dramatic rise in their employment by big companies looking to improve their bottom lines.[3] Procurement consultants are not persuaded by your solution's benefits. Their charter isn't connected to business progress—they are 100% focused on "extracting maximum value from the purchase decision." They are usually compensated based on the savings that are achieved between your quote and the final price their clients pay, leading to high-pressure negotiating tactics and routine audits of prior deals to "uncover grounds for renegotiation."[4] As mercenaries, they are far removed from the value of your solutions or, for that matter, the pain your prospects are trying to solve. These cost terminators are immune to any emotional appeals and in many cases must be neutralized in order for you to profitably do business with your prospect.

The second driver of complexity in the selling landscape is the fact that today's prospects have abundant information at their fingertips to assist them throughout their buying journey. With the advent of self-service research, the tables have turned on the B2B seller, who previously drove the conversation by being the sole party doling out key information about the market, the product, and its comparative benefits.

When the Corporate Executive Board and Google conducted a survey of buyers throughout business-to-business circles, they confirmed this drastic shift. "Sellers today face not only higher deal complexity and increased variability, but also better-informed customers who are engaging suppliers much later in the purchase process. . . . Customers on average have completed nearly 60% of their purchasing decision before having a conversation with a supplier. . . . For many organizations, the sales playbook has to be completely rewritten to compete effectively."[5]

With the power of search engines, proprietary information archives and the corporate intranet, your buyers don't need you to "detail" them anymore. They think they understand their pain, the set of alternatives available, and even what you should charge. No longer can you create the awareness of the problem and then reveal your solution, triggering an "aha" moment where doing a deal becomes a no-brainer for the buyer. The psychology of the sale has changed entirely.

Of course, this assumes the prospect's research is spot on, which isn't usually the case. "In many situations, the quality of the information they get is suspect. Many times it's a blogger who either has half the story or a highly specific situation where he's generalized to the whole industry," says Cox Media Group executive Paul Curran. "Half of the battle for us is to reeducate the prospect based on data that actually applies to their situation." While your sales development team can separate the facts from the link baiters, your prospect may not.

The new world of everything's online has also made it harder for us to justify our price points, especially if what we sell is value added. In the automotive buying space, services like TrueCar have armed consumers with transparent pricing data, giving them the ability to negotiate the sale down to breakeven for many dealers. The world has gotten tougher on everything from value justification to making a profitable sale. For other goods, Amazon and eBay provide buyers instant estimates of the worth of any item they are considering.

You might think these examples don't apply to business-to-business sales. But in reality, a buyer is a buyer, and in today's world we all search our way to wisdom, whether as individual consumers or large companies. Researchers at Avanade recently reported that today's business buyers are "mimicking consumer shopping behaviors," blurring the lines between B2B and B2C.[6] This is why you should follow developments in how consumers find, vet, and buy products. It's only a matter of time before these data- and web-powered techniques make their way into your sales process.

The third cause of sales complexity is a result of the nature of what most of us are selling these days: an increasingly technical set of products and services. As companies' problems have magnified in a digital, mobile, 24/7/365 world, we've answered the bell by developing cutting-edge solutions that require computer science and business school degrees to comprehend. It's no surprise buyers are building teams and doing their homework to keep up with the pace of progress.

In the case of Skillsoft, consumers aren't interested in just purchasing low-technology training products. Videos are now distributed through online learning management systems that rival SAP supply-chain software in their feature set. These sophisticated systems suggest content to employees based on their stated needs or managerial assessments, a far cry from the old-fashioned TV and tape player on a stand solution from years gone by.

As the products get more complicated, communicating what they do and how they deliver value gets harder, too. The learning curve for the sales rep goes up sharply. With each new product rollout, there's more to keep up with and then, in turn, relay to a variety of buyers all from different walks of business life.

The fourth development adding to the degree of deal difficulty is the proliferation of competitors enabled by the rapidly falling costs of launching a startup. Thanks to the cloud, the crowd, and off-the-shelf digital technology, the number of competitors chipping away at your territory is growing exponentially.

This is why one of the toughest sales challenges we face today is retaining our current book of business. Whether we have a gap in service or need to maintain or increase our prices to keep up with costs, there's always a new kid on the block ready to swoop in and serve your customers for cheap or even free.

When I started selling media, there were only a few radio stations in town and the local newspaper. That was the range of options my prospects had to choose from. When I joined Yahoo! in 2000, there were only a few other website publishers with the volume of traffic that could entice major advertisers. Today, there are hundreds of major web publishers and countless ad networks that aggregate audiences. As the barriers to entry continue to drop and targeting allows niche players to compete at a high level, it's truly a multiplayer game for marketing solution providers.

For those selling technology services, rapid app development combined with cloud computing has changed the game when it comes to selling software or hardware. Enterprise-wide annual or multiyear licenses are rare, with many companies buying pay-as-you-go services from startups. Computer equipment deals are slimmed down as well, as companies realize the value of using cloud services to drive down costs. Buying small or "just in time" has become the order of the day.

Up until now, I've focused on how the average business solution sale is getting much tougher. When it comes to the big wins—those that have a significant impact on your company's revenue or market position—the difficulty level rises even more. Take the high-revenue sale, for example. Whether it's several hundred thousand dollars for a software utility or several million dollars for a business process out-sourcing arrangement, there is a lot of risk in the proposition of mak-ing these huge deals while we're still smarting from the last recession and bombarded with headlines about the next one on the way.

This instability has ignited a level of uncertainty throughout many prospect companies, which increases the number of players on the buyer's deal team as well as the tendency to look under every rock and research every cranny. Big deals are sold in adversarial situations, in most cases. The prospect has heard it all before, and the seller pitches in quicksand while the chances of success sink with every passing moment.

Even if you succeed in winning over all of the stakeholders, there's still the pesky issue of getting the megadeal contract signed. Due to legislation like Sarbanes-Oxley (a 2002 federal law expanding gover-nance requirements for public companies) and increasingly active boards, there is more scrutiny over corporate governance than ever before. Dan Veitkus, who has led enterprise sales teams over the last few decades at Novell and Progress Software, has ample experience with getting zapped at the finish line. "Across the board, we've seen a lower threshold of signature authority implemented in companies of all sizes. There used to be a time when a director could sign a million-dollar deal, but today, that needs to also be signed off on by the CFO and the CEO." When climbing that far up the ladder, the game usually starts all over again for your sales team.

Sometimes a big win is that multimillion- or billion-dollar win that determines your company's whole year. Another corporate big win, however, is successfully planting a flag in a new territory or an industry niche. Those who can get there first have the best shot at being a leader in the space. For many startups, or even new business units, like Oracle's CX team, getting the first best foot in the market is the key.

Neil Miklusak manages a team that sells advertising solutions for LinkedIn. While LinkedIn does a brisk business helping staffing companies and hiring managers find talent, its display advertising business is not yet a mainstream option for financial services firms such as T. Rowe Price, Bank of America, and J.P. Morgan, which currently prefer to advertise on publisher websites like Yahoo!, The Motley Fool, and Bloomberg News. "Financial services firms are risk averse when it comes to these things," Neil told me. "Their industry is complicated by compliance regulations, which makes this whole social media space a gray area to them."

In other words, it's a market of wait and see, which is why it's such a big opportunity for social media publishers that land the beachhead deal. Prospects have no case study that's apples to apples by which to make a safe bet. They believe that pioneers get arrows in their backs, so they adopt the best-to-market approach and wait it out while the startups and innovators starve.

Those buying the unknown or, even worse, buying the risky, add more levels to the process, more hoops for the deal makers to jump through. This turns what should be a presentation, demo, and test-then-scale process into a mountain-climbing expedition for the seller. As TrueCar founder Scott Painter once told me: "When you are the new, getting from zero to one is half the journey. It's that hard in the beginning."

More than ever, though, we need to chase the big or the groundbreaking deals to survive. For mature enterprises or companies selling business solutions in mature markets, winning the enterprise-wide deal creates a pipeline of future success and builds a real barrier to entry for your competitors.

In *Mastering the Complex Sale*, Jeff Thull sounded a clarion call to B2B companies that weren't pursuing the tough sale. "The restructuring of organizations has extended up and down the supply chain," he wrote. "Customers are consolidating, few companies are controlling higher percentages of supply. . . . If your customers are tightening up their supply chains, there will be fewer sales opportunities. Further, one lost sale in the chain could easily translate into the long-term loss of a customer."[7]

In other words, there are a lot less fish in the sea, and they are grouping in schools that will be harder than ever to net. Those with the ambition to cast widely and dive deeply will take all. You've got to pursue the biggest of the biggest to compete.

For startups, cracking into a market needs to happen almost immediately. Venture capital professionals have numerous options for investments, and with lower costs of entry, they are waiting out the market to see who can get the big wins. Even if you can land seed funding, without overcoming pioneer phobia in your market, you'll eventually miss payroll when your next round fails to close.

If you work in a new business unit or venture operation at a big company, next year's budget is no sure thing. Public companies are spinning off or abandoning new product extensions faster than ever as a result of increasing investor activism that pressures them to protect the cash cow.[8]

Even though the big ones are the toughest to win, you really have no choice but to grit your teeth and go after them anyway.

For some, this is depressing, just as much as the fact that 40% of sales reps today fail to make quota, a startling decrease of almost 20% over the last decade. For others (like you), it's a game-changing opportunity to stand out as a sales leader or top contributor. The trick is to have the vision and strategy in place—and the process to follow through and break through on the big wins.

Though the challenges I've outlined are serious, they are not insurmountable. Through collaboration, you can stay one step ahead of the game. It's a matter of joining forces with others and approaching complexity from all sides, which brings me back to the world of gaming.

As video games became tougher to beat—seemingly impossible, at times—players started to plot against game makers to level the playing field. As early as 1983, with the ZX Spectrum *Manic Miner* game, hackers reimagined how to play the game by doing research on programming developments and comparing notes and sharing cheat codes with other players.[9] They worked with competitors, strangers, and people from other parts of the world to produce publications to gang up on the game makers, often outnumbering them. They were lavish with praise and recognition for those who made level-busting contributions. They learned new ways to use their controllers and developed new logic to counter the programmer's ever-changing set of obstacles. Through collaboration, they significantly reduced the time it took to complete even the most difficult games.

Their insight is yours: *When the going gets tough, the ambitious get innovative.*

In this book, I'll show you how to respond to your rising sales challenges just like the hackers did to theirs. While they didn't have a process per se, they applied systems thinking at every step of the way. I'll show you how to do your own reconnaissance on the playing field, isolating exactly where you are stuck in the sales process and why. That critical first step will help you determine whom you need to join forces with in order to move forward in your sales challenge.

You'll learn how to onboard your new team members, briefing them on the state of the game and giving them specific parts of the challenge to solve. I'll reveal meeting facilitation techniques that will help them compare notes, combine ideas, and build workarounds and weapons of deal progress. In the end, you'll figure out how to share these breakthroughs throughout your company, converting complexity into a brutal competitive advantage.

But first, you'll need to shake off two myths of creativity and innovation that will trap you in your quest to solve the complex. These myths cause most to look for "moon shot" ideas from individual geniuses, which, as you'll see, is the wrong approach.

CHAPTER 2

A Thousand Problems Solved

Several years ago, I met Pixar cofounder and president Ed Catmull when we were both asked to participate at a Disney corporate leadership event in Orlando. Disney was one of our top clients at Yahoo! as well as Pixar's most important business partner.

Although Ed was soft spoken, his demeanor signaled that he was approachable, so I talked him up while we were backstage. His sense of style reminded me of Steve Jobs: black shirt underneath a sport jacket, wire-frame glasses, and a salt-and-pepper beard. He asked me a few questions about Yahoo!, and in turn I asked him questions about the making of *Toy Story,* one of my favorite movies of all time.

"The movie was groundbreaking," I said. "I laughed, I cried . . . and all in response to computer-generated characters. Your John Lasseter [*Toy Story*'s director] is a genius for coming up with the twist of telling the story from the toys' point of view. What an achievement in creative thinking!"

He acknowledged the originality of the script, but he told me it was a very difficult movie to make, ticking off numerous obstacles and complications that immediately cropped up in production. He explained that Lasseter and his team faced creative, technological, and financial challenges at every step of the way. At times, he said, he wondered whether the movie would actually get made.

In no way was his dismissive response a slight of Lasseter or his script. Catmull's statement was really a description of the ginormous challenge they faced in attempting to make the first full-length motion picture in a computer and not losing their shirts.

Bringing Lasseter's vision to life posed ascending levels of challenge throughout the movie-making process, from scripting to editing to distribution. The Pixar team rebooted story development more than once. To make characters emotive, they had to develop thousands of facial motion controllers. To render the movie in a reasonable period of time, they had to figure out how to synchronize hundreds of Sun servers, and keep them running around the clock. It was an arduous five-year journey for team Pixar.

"*Toy Story*," Catmull said, "was a thousand problems solved."

That statement resonated with something I'd witnessed in my sales life: a done deal is a host of problems solved. And many of these problems are internal to your company, based on its policies or defined sales process. For the biggest deals, dozens, if not hundreds, of problems must be overcome to secure a signature on the final contract.

Previously, I thought that big deals were cracked by a thunderbolt of lightning, a big idea falling out of the sky and into the head of the genius salesperson or manager. After all, big deals are really big ideas realized, right?

Not so. According to creativity expert Robert Weisberg, the big idea is one of the myths of genius. His exhaustive research finds that most great inventors merely solved the last problem, enabling an existing solution to achieve mainstream adoption. Charles Darwin didn't come up with the theory of evolution; he found a way to eloquently explain the process of natural selection, which helped the scientific community finally accept the fact that humans evolved over time. Eli

Whitney didn't invent the cotton gin in one day after watching a cat trying to pull a chicken through a fence unsuccessfully, as the story goes. Instead, he adapted existing gin technology to work on short-staple cotton, which was abundant in supply. He, too, was a problem solver, not a conduit of divine inspiration. The same applies to the inventions and discoveries of Edison, Newton, and Franklin.[1]

This reinforces my perspective that each member of a dealstorm needs to be a tenacious problem solver and not someone waiting for breakthrough ideas to save the day. In dealstorms I've led and consulted on, we've slashed our way through obstacles, hazards, puzzles, and conundrums that lie between the prospective idea and the brag-worthy accomplishment. We didn't wait on the eureka moment to happen; we plugged away at solving problems, big and small. We took control of the process and won many more deals, no muse required.

In the world of complex sales, you must ascend levels from initial contact to signed contract and contend with many obstacles at each stage. In my experience, there are four major levels we must conquer to win:

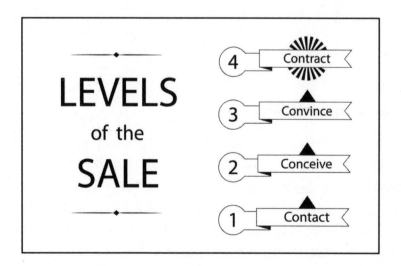

LEVELS
of the
SALE

4 Contract

3 Convince

2 Conceive

1 Contact

➤ **Contact:** Our first level involves engaging with all necessary informers, influencers, mobilizers, or decision makers at the prospect company.

➤ **Conceive:** This is where the vision of how your company can add value is created. Based on information you collect concerning the prospect's problems and the knowledge you possess about your company's capabilities, you come up with a win-win selling proposition.

➤ **Convince:** At this level, you move the prospects to act on your recommendation. Often, you provide them with ammunition to sell your proposal forward to other influencers or deciders you'll never meet.

➤ **Contract:** The final step is to consummate the relationship with a firm and binding commitment to buy your solution.

As you navigate these levels, there are tough challenges that will bog down your journey and, in some cases, defeat you entirely. There is no ultraweapon or shield that gives you superpowers in this arena or grants you immunity. Your success depends on your ability to solve problems quickly, before the window of opportunity closes for you and your company.

The Contact Level

The first challenge of this level is to identify your point of contact. Gone are the days of prospecting based on calling the CEO or business owner listed on a Dun & Bradstreet lead card. There are no current organizational charts or budget-spender directories available to make this easy for you. While social media resources like LinkedIn and search engines like Google give you a starting point, they aren't always up to date or accurate. Networking is still the best way to figure out the decision-making web at a prospect company.

Once you have prospective contacts in your crosshairs, the next challenge is to engage them, which involves breaking through screens (read: assistants) or the clutter of requests for their attention. Don't forget that your competitors are also constantly clamoring for their attention—and that the prospect company is also likely already doing its own research, too.

In the past, one only had to call on a specific person, usually the business owner, company president, or the relevant department director, as the main contact for a sale. But as we explored in the last chapter, today that department director or company president is only one connection in a web of internal decision makers and influencers.

In many situations, your initial contact serves as a stepping stone to key influencers or the ultimate decision makers. The higher up you have to go, the bigger the barriers to connection are. In most cases, you'll need to figure out how to make this leap without offending your original contacts. Or, like Dan Craig at Oracle, you might need to move from dealing with your initial information technology contact to a business manager who has budget and interest in the software solution you are selling. Although this is a lateral move, and maybe you'll get an assist from your new buddy in IT, it still requires you to adapt to the new perspectives and needs of your next target.

If you are trying to bring back an account you've lost, you'll have to reestablish contact, which can be difficult if your company didn't deliver value as promised. If you clashed with your key contact or rubbed him the wrong way, you'll likely need to branch out, making new friends in high places to earn your second chance. In some cases, you might be best served to attempt contact with an entirely new group of influencers or decision makers. But even if you accomplish that, there's still the likelihood that your reputation will precede you.

Breaking through the contact level involves intense research as well as the ability to plumb deeply into the organization to connect with everyone who has a stake in the buy.

The Conceive Level

Deal conception starts with a deep level of product knowledge. Beyond your sales collateral, you need to understand how your product works, where it came from, and what its true capabilities are. You'll need to ask associates more questions about product functionality than you're used to if you want to develop an intuition about how your company can truly serve others. Like TV detective Columbo, you'll need to possess enough humility to go back to the well and ask "one more stupid question."

Next, you must learn about your prospect's business situation in order to locate the relevant pain points. If you can't find the burning need, you'll never develop the required urgency to move the game along. In some cases, you'll need to understand the company's history, how it makes money, and what its strategy is for the future. This is rarely evident from the outside, so you'll need to coax your contacts into educating you about their situation. Don't expect them to want to do it, though. Not only do they easily grow tired of repeating themselves, in many cases they don't really know the answers. Sometimes they will withhold information from you as a form of leverage. After all, why do they want to give you the upper hand?

Once informed of their addressable problems, you'll need to position the prospect against your company's products to find relevant examples of success. It's rare to pluck a product off the shelf and hatch the deal. Your next challenge is to thoroughly understand all of your company's capabilities and its willingness to customize, prototype, or partner its way into a winning solution.

In many situations, if the pain points are big enough, the buyers are already on their solution-finding journey. In this case, you need to understand where they are in the process as well as what research they've done and how it affects their purchasing perspective. Many prospects will appreciate your sensitivity to the work they've already done and will enthuse at how your proposal is coming along at the right time.

The last hurdle you face at this stage is pricing the deal to create a win for the prospect as well as a profit for your company. While there are some metrics available to give you guidance, fuzzy math is more common. In the end, you'll be tasked with a best guess that will likely frame the deal more than the features and benefits you will tout at the next level of the game.

The Convince Level

Any solution you sell requires a prospect to change how it does business in some way. Whether it's accepting and acclimating to a new process, new vendor, or new technology, convincing the prospect to buy in to the unknown is an uphill battle.

First, you must demonstrate that you can solve the prospect company's problem and give a high return on investment, which usually means taking costs out of its system or boosting effectiveness of its strategy in a measurable way. Your demo may wow, but it's not proof of your product's utility for them. Your case studies may impress, but they aren't always seen as relevant to the prospect's situation. Your success predictions, and the assumptions behind them, will be questioned. Presumption lies with the status quo.

Next, you'll need to convince the prospects that your company is uniquely suited to solve this problem—better than the incumbent they work with or the dozen other providers they have already found. For startups, new business divisions, or companies with not-so-perfect histories, this can be a herculean task.

Even when you've got their heads nodding, that doesn't mean they are going to move to action any time soon. You'll need to instill a sense of urgency to move forward; otherwise, you'll get stuck in a repeating cycle of happy talk. At the opposite end of the spectrum is uncertainty, especially when they consider technical, financial, or political side effects of adopting your solution.

Finally, you'll need to employ a persuasion device (formula, metaphor, illustration, etc.) that resonates and persuades every influencer, procurement lead, and contract signer—even when you aren't around to present to them individually.

The Contract Level

During this final level, you will encounter a new force: the legal group. The more complex your contract, the longer this group will take to review it and return it to you. There can be days or weeks of latency between each iteration of the agreement, and the urgency you established at the convince level won't necessarily resonate with the people responsible for contracting. While you may be able to marshal your contacts to pressure them for a faster response, they are often beholden to the whims of their general counsel as well.

During contract review, there can be sticking points in terms and conditions. In some cases, you are navigating the prospect's policies and procedures; in other situations, you are lobbying to your internal legal group to accept the prospect's counteroffers.

Often the payment terms create a skirmish between the prospect's way of doing business and your company's. This can trigger the involvement of a procurement group, which, of course, can create even more delays and additional layers of friction to overcome.

Problem solving isn't always direct. Often we are navigating the prospect's culture, or how things are done there. The prospect company has a process for how it wants sellers to engage with it (and you don't know it going in). Most prospect companies maintain secrecy about how they do business when it comes to outsiders or vendors. Some have a way of measuring value that is idiosyncratic and secret. Others might prefer to do business with a deal memo, purchase order, or a handshake. In order to ascend to the top level of the game, you have to clear all of these hurdles.

And please remember: time is not on your side. If you take too long to conceive, convince, or contract, your key contacts may leave the company, be transferred to a new group, or be promoted out of the division. Worse, the prospect company may be acquired, which hits the reset button on everything. In that case, much like a video game, you will have to start over at some lower level.

Hardcore closing techniques may have sped things up back in the day when you were selling the only game in town to an addressable decision maker. But now, you'll have to be nuanced so as to keep the deal moving along quickly without ticking off someone and blowing up the foundation of your deal—the relationship. That's why success comes down to your ability to solve problems faster than your competition—and in a way that builds progress with the prospect at every step.

But not to fear: if you approach your next sales challenge with the dealstorming process in your pocket, you'll move through each level, solving problems incrementally and methodically.

CHAPTER 3

Sales Genius Is a Team Sport

I n the game of enterprise sales, completing a multimillion-dollar deal requires building diverse and engaged teams. There will be a series of obstacles at each level of the sale, often thrown in your way by people you've never encountered before. The vision that lands the relationship with a company isn't usually wide enough to elevate it into a strategic partnership. Clever, creative, and brilliant moves will be required and likely can't be made by a small group from the same department. Consider the following example, which illustrates this point powerfully.

Alyssa DeMattos, an account executive at online job site and employer talent solutions company CareerBuilder, thinks of her company's relationship with staffing industry leader Allegis as a love story. True to the archetypal plot, their connection has had its ups and downs. For years, Allegis was a major customer of CareerBuilder, buying their core products such as access to résumés and media promoting its staffing opportunities. But in 2008, the two companies "broke up" as a result of a contentious disagreement about a significant rate increase. Eric Gilpin, president of CareerBuilder's staffing and recruiting group, decided to wait a few years before attempting to resurrect the account. In 2011, he selected Alyssa as the new account executive tasked with wooing Allegis back. He trusted her and knew that if anyone could bring Allegis back, she could.

Alyssa quickly learned that one of the reasons their relationship ended was that Allegis felt betrayed by CareerBuilder. Because the previous rep had relationships with only a few people inside one of the many business units at Allegis, the near doubling of their advertising and services rates came as a shock to the dozens of users throughout the company and the president of their biggest division. It escalated into a contentious phone call between him and CareerBuilder's CEO, Matt Ferguson, which resulted in the termination of their relationship.

Winning back their trust wouldn't be easy. Over the next year, Alyssa met with, listened to, and gave free advice to leaders and managers across Allegis. She became a trusted resource to a key Allegis executive who, in turn, gave her insight into the company and its changing needs. Eventually, Alyssa was given the chance to bring back the business via a side-by-side test with Monster, which had stepped in after the breakup. In 2012, CareerBuilder was awarded a contract with Allegis that was over three times larger than the one that fizzled out four years earlier.

While Alyssa was thrilled about the deal, she knew that the two companies could grow even closer in the coming years.

Around that time, CareerBuilder was making a big shift from media company (as a job board that aggregated an audience of job seekers) to technology solutions company. At a sales kickoff, Alyssa heard her CEO speak about his vision for the company's future, in which he detailed the tens of millions of dollars they were investing in acquisitions as well as head count at their Atlanta technology hub. He admonished sales reps to find opportunities where CareerBuilder could leverage their software programming, data, and website design capabilities into sticky, game-changing opportunities with their biggest clients.

Ever the matchmaker, Alyssa realized that Allegis was a perfect fit for this opportunity. It occurred to her that if any company could benefit from CareerBuilder's move into Big Data and software as a service (SaaS), it would be Allegis. She canvassed her legion of friends at Allegis, only to find out that they had never outsourced critical technology solutions, so convincing them to "let go" was an exponentially more complex process than unseating Monster for staffing placement services.

As Alyssa soon realized, the only way to deliver her CEO's vision, in which customers would be married at the server with CareerBuilder, would be to fan out the dealstorming process across the enterprise. If she could bring enough minds together through collaboration, team genius would make a deal with Allegis happen. What she didn't count on was having to spend so much time and effort recruiting her dealstorm team and then getting them to jump through dozens of hoops over a protracted period of time.

Allegis differentiates itself in the staffing services market with its technology, including a multimillion-dollar applicant tracking system that their IT team built from scratch. Allegis trusted few, if any, outsiders to do its important engineering or development work.

Though they had successfully signed the deal CareerBuilder set out to make, Alyssa believed that Allegis was missing a key functionality that CareerBuilder could provide. From content creation to data-driven automation to website management, she knew there was a big opportunity for the two companies to partner on a career site for the hundreds of thousands of people in their staffing talent network. It was a matter of getting Allegis to show her what it had under the hood.

Alyssa quickly realized how difficult it would be to pry this information loose from Allegis, so she formed a dealstorm team to strategize on how to get the discovery process going and move through each level of the sale. The team—which consisted of the divisional president, her manager, and the account coordinator—came up with the idea to host a technology best practices meeting, where technology leads from Allegis and CareerBuilder would share their strategies, demo recent projects, and discuss how trends in technology would affect them in the future. No selling, just comparing notes.

First, Alyssa needed a participation commitment from her IT team in Atlanta. So she hit up CareerBuilder's chief of technology, Eric Presley, someone she'd never met or talked to. She cold called Presley to sell him on hosting the meeting and assigning several of his technical leads to copresent. She explained how Allegis and CareerBuilder delivered staffing solutions in a similar way and that exposure of his staff to their top IT managers would be a collaborative win-win. Per Alyssa, she "sold him on the dream" of a new CareerBuilder that powered the candidate experience for companies as a critical services provider and not just a job board.

Impressed with her pitch, Eric gave the green light for the meeting and committed to his group's participation. At this point, he and a handful of his group leaders were pulled into the dealstorm in the middle of the conceive phase.

Alyssa paid careful attention to every detail around the Atlanta summit. She staged a dinner the night before the meeting, setting the table with napkins custom printed to read, "CareerBuilder Loves Allegis." She produced a branded journal for them to take notes in during the meeting. She even planned the snacks her guests would eat the next day.

Alyssa is a big fan of baked goods, especially cupcakes. She arranged for a local bakery to make cupcakes with candy hearts on top that read, "CareerBuilder Loves Allegis." Andrea, her manager, picked up the cupcakes the morning of the summit. But when they opened the box, only minutes before the meeting would begin, they discovered that the bakery produced only half of the order. They would have only a dozen cupcakes for over two dozen attendees. Alyssa put out the cupcakes in front of the project leads, who started to joke that though the cupcakes were delicious, they were going to run out before everyone got to try one.

At the meeting, as members were buzzing about the cupcakes, CareerBuilder engineers presented their newest tools and system developments. Alyssa noted that the Allegis participants repeatedly remarked, "We don't have that piece of the puzzle!" when CareerBuilder showed them an element of their tech capabilities that Allegis didn't yet have. This is when Alyssa put a creative twist on the situation. The cupcake shortage, she explained, represented the situation Allegis had with their homegrown candidate experience system. The bakery didn't have the right system in place to consistently deliver on their orders, she said. The same was true for the Allegis side, where someone there wasn't getting "cupcakes" from the IT team. Without the data-driven back end that CareerBuilder offered, many of Allegis's clients would experience shortages of staff—a shortage of cupcakes—to fill clients' requisitions.

The "cupcake shortage" analogy had a visceral impact on the Allegis team, helping them to truly grasp the potential of a partnership. They opened up to the CareerBuilder team's proposition. By the end of the day, they revealed details about a robust career site project they had planned to build themselves.

At this point, they were so impressed with CareerBuilder's tech team, the meeting morphed into a collaborative product design planning meeting—where an Allegis executive bluntly asked Alyssa, "Couldn't *you* build this for us?"

"That's when we figured out the real deal," Alyssa explained. "If we built, hosted, and fueled their career portal, we'd be their partner for a long time." Not only would it boost CareerBuilder's pivot into technology services, it would be the largest deal in the company's history. But it would not come easy.

Although Allegis's IT managers were impressed with what they saw that day, they were still highly risk averse when it came to their technology. They issued a request for proposals (RFP) within a few weeks to CareerBuilder and over a dozen other technology vendors.

To win the day, Alyssa would need to sway what she called "a tribe of Allegis stakeholders," including managers from regional divisions, finance, marketing, operations, technology, and business operations, and convince them that CareerBuilder was the best partner above all the competition.

Back in her office, Alyssa reviewed the dealstorm team she had assembled. She added a marketing manager to the team to bring insights to the presentation process and build elements for their upcoming presentation at Allegis headquarters in Baltimore. In a subsequent meeting, this expanded dealstorm team conjured up the idea of producing a video telling the product story from the candidate's point of view, making the point that only a leader in job placement like CareerBuilder could truly understand the end user.

The presentation went well and when Allegis announced the three finalists, CareerBuilder made the list, though their rival Monster was also still in the running. The stakes couldn't be higher. This would be a winner-take-all deal. Whoever would build the career site would also get the core listings and résumé access business. That meant Alyssa would lose the entire account if her team didn't win. There were millions of reasons for her to get highly motivated.

To be convinced, though, Allegis needed to try before they signed. It turned out CareerBuilder was the only finalist that didn't have a working prototype of a site for them to test drive. Although Career-Builder's engineers had built many career sites to date, none of them had the size, scale, and functionality of the one that they were proposing to Allegis. When Alyssa revealed this to one of her key contacts, he replied, "You are selling vapor!" She knew that to convince Allegis of their competency, they'd have to build a prototype just for them.

Eight engineers would have to come off their projects for six weeks to build the prototype. Furthermore, she wanted them to give the

Allegis IT team a developer key so "they could bang on the prototype and make it their own."

At this point, with so much on the line, all the company's engineers were heads down, building CareerBuilder's Talent Network, a major project that was also part of the CEO's vision for the future. The director of the project shot down the request for a prototype build, offering instead to deliver a handful of mock-ups and screen shots for her final presentation. "That would not work," Alyssa said. "I would not take no for an answer!"

Even though the Allegis career site project had a lot of upside for the company, CareerBuilder's chief technology officer, Eric Presley, was constrained in terms of head count, and his team was already overwhelmed. During an hour-long phone call, Alyssa peppered him with questions about the Talent Network, its functionality, and how his team conducted quality control. (Later, he told Eric Gilpin that he respected how many questions she asked.)

To sway him to pull people off other projects and onto this prototype, Alyssa explained that she would collect immediate feedback from the Allegis IT team on functionality, which could in turn reduce the cycle time for his Talent Network build. By giving his engineers direct access to a live client, they would receive instant gratification for programming and engineering work they were doing. It made sense to Presley, as there was no other feedback loop set up to vet his team's project for real client user experience. Believing that the prototype project fit within the Talent Network road map, he approved the build. Alyssa didn't take their involvement for granted, either. She explained to each engineer the strategic value of the project and surprised them with lunch as they worked on the prototype.

When Alyssa and her team presented a live demo of the Allegis career site prototype on pitch day, she explained how they had diverted precious resources in quest of this opportunity. After revealing a slide charting up-and-down relationships, culminating with a prototype along with a developer key, she declared, "It's time for us to get married."

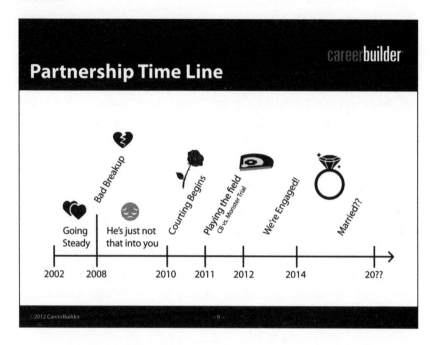

Within a few weeks, she received great news: CareerBuilder won the competition, and it was time to move to contract.

Then they came to a hitch in the last level of the sale: payment terms. By policy, Allegis paid for projects upon completion. The problem for CareerBuilder was that it would take at least six months to complete the build, and by their policy, that would be too long to wait on any form of payment.

"What Allegis needed to see was work they could touch," Alyssa said. So, in collaboration with legal, finance, and HR, they came up with another solution. CareerBuilder would hire a tech-savvy project manager the day the contract was signed to provide concierge-level services to Allegis, "officing" at their headquarters in Baltimore.

This new provision would increase the contract price by one hundred thousand dollars but would expedite the build and ensure real-time feedback. This creative move signaled to Allegis that work would be delivered from day one, and CareerBuilder would immediately have to allocate cash to consummate the relationship and ensure its health.

With this addition in place, Allegis signed the contract, including advance payment. The marriage was made. Today, the two companies are closer than ever—as are the collaborators on each side that made the deal happen. Mike McSally, vice president of enterprise operations at Allegis, even sent Alyssa flowers on Christmas Eve in 2014 as a token of his appreciation for their relationship. When she was given the account opportunity in 2011, Mike was the key person who had to be persuaded to give CareerBuilder another chance. Alyssa tenaciously pursued building a relationship with him by offering valuable advice, humility, and a dab of her charm. Mike and CareerBuilder's CEO play golf together when they get a chance. The deal was successfully contracted and conceived, Allegis convinced, and contract reached thanks to Alyssa's persistence in applying dealstorming practices and process to all stages of the sale.

"That deal put us in the billion-dollar annual revenue category," says divisional president Eric Gilpin. "And it was classic Alyssa. Whenever you put obstacles in her way, she digs in, asks questions, recruits coconspirators, and finds a way to win."

In the course of writing this book, I interviewed over two hundred sales leaders about their most innovative deal-making situations. In many instances, the stories they first shared revolved around a single person and his or her breakthrough creativity.

The idea of a lone genius is a romantic notion, really: a single person, working alone, receives divine inspiration and through grit and determination changes the world. "We want to believe that seemingly unique inventions and creations are the product of a sole creator," explained David Burkus, former pharmaceutical sales representative and now college professor and author of *The Myths of Creativity*. "When we have a creative idea, we want the world to recognize us as the genius we are, so we, in turn, recognize others as sole geniuses behind their great ideas."

In other words, our desire to be recognized as individuals makes us buy in to the illusion that individuals produce acts of genius. "It's part of how we are wired to think," David told me. "The hero's journey is part of mythology. People love to talk about Steve Jobs as the genius inventor, but often they don't talk about the other Steve [Wozniak], Jony Ive, or Tony Fadell. They are in the footnotes of most conversations."

This mythology was promoted by early creativity research, which diligently focused on the individual genius, his or her background, and the unique working environments, which led to breakthrough thinking. But as more social scientists and psychologists entered the field, new facts emerged about how genius actually manifests. "Beginning in the 1990s, our research began to point in the opposite direction," writes University of North Carolina professor Keith Sawyer in his book *Group Genius*. "We began to see that innovations once believed to be the creation of the genius actually emerged from invisible collaborations, and the collaboration was responsible for famous creations throughout history." In his book, he explains how "Thomas Edison" is considered a collective noun in the industry, representing over a dozen people he worked with. "We screw in light bulbs today because one of Edison's lab assistants saw Edison cleaning his hands with turpentine; when the inventor unscrewed the metal top of the metal can, the assistant had the idea of the screw-in lamp base."[1]

The popular trope doesn't match the truth. The solo inventor is a better story, so that's how it gets told around the campfire and in most books. And in most companies, too. We love to praise our rock stars more than account for our bricklayers. But often, when I dug into the stories in this book and talked directly to the people at the center of the deals themselves, it turned out the lone sales genius wasn't really so alone. He or she was working in a collective environment where multiple players built on observations, improved on ideas, and worked together as a team. While the account executive owned the problem, the team produced the true genius.

There is no lone genius in sales. No individual account executive or sales manager makes the big deal or saves the strategic account on his own. Lone genius isn't the difference maker in closing complex sales. The source of true innovation is teamwork. As Sawyer says, "Collaborative webs are more important than creative people."[2]

Let that sink in for a second: groups of regular folk working together as a team trump innovative thinkers. Wow. If you're a sales leader, this should change your mental model for recruiting. In this complicated selling environment, you should stop focusing on hiring "top producers" and, instead, search out and acquire team players with the tendency to spin up webs to capture sales opportunities.

There's another reason this loner superstar myth needs to vanish from sales culture: we need to proactively pursue collaboration and not look at it as a last resort option when best individual efforts aren't enough. Through his work with companies and organizations, David Burkus came to the same conclusion: "If we believe that innovation is a solo effort, then we're more likely to remove ourselves from the networks we need." When it comes to problem solving, your network truly is your net worth.

Genius is in the process that creates a remarkable work, enabled by a collection of people working together. It starts with a commitment to solve a problem, an observation that leads to an idea, improvements to the idea, and then, of course, relentless execution. A single person cannot complete this process. It takes a team.

If you think your sales department is already working as a team, I have a question for you: Is it a tall team or a wide team? This is an important distinction and yet another fallacy of thought in sales leadership circles.

When your team is vertically organized to include sales leaders, managers, reps, enablement, account management, and sales training, that's not a collaborative web—that's a silo. It's a collection of people steeped in sales-think, which is usually pretty insular. The sales silo sees other groups around the company as either service providers or "the land of no."

Yup, I said it: sales builds silos, often hardened to protect them from the outside world. In fact, according to several prominent CEOs I've talked to, sales is as bad at building silos as product groups or brand teams. One reason for this self-selective insulation is that many account executives find it difficult to give up any level of control over the selling process because they fear that collaborating with other departments could lead to them having an equal say in what can be sold, and how. Further, many in the sales department believe they know the customer better than anyone else in the company because they talk to the customer every day.

However, your dealstorming team will not be complete unless you create a wide team to diversify the mix and, most important, cover up any holes or blind spots that can lead to an easy win for the competition. Think of it this way: If your football team consisted of a quarterback, three running backs, six wide receivers, and two tight ends, who would block? Who would play defense? Who would kick off or attempt field goals? You'd field an offense-only football team.

You will struggle to solve your sales challenges if you are concentrated on the sales side of the ball in building your dealstorming team. A bunch of people in the sales world will think, well, like salespeople. You'll lack key insights that affect the value of what you sell, how profitable it will be, how it will resonate through the prospect company, and, most important, whether you can actually deliver on what you sell.

To actually get the benefits of the dealstorming team, you must create a wide team like Alyssa DeMattos did, breaking organizational boundaries and ensnaring unlikely players, such as cross-country engineering groups or customer champions. The wider your team is, the stronger the collaborative web becomes.

Aerospace and transportation company Bombardier responds to deals "stuck in the pipeline" by employing what it refers to as peer consulting cohorts. According to CEB's Jessica Williams, this group of managers, from across various business units, "push each other's thinking and develop approaches to real-world business problems."[3] This combination has led to a competitive advantage in multiplayer bid situations in which billions of dollars are on the line for those who weave the right approach.

Like Bombardier, when a B2B sales culture embraces the team sport of problem solving, companies usually become winners in their market, or "world-class performers," according to a 2014 study by research group Miller Heiman Research Institute.[4] World-class sales performers are defined as companies that outperform their rivals by an average of 20% across key metrics such as new account acquisition or average account billing over a protracted period of time. When Miller Heiman analyzed what separated these companies from the pack, "conscious collaboration" emerged as the decisive factor.

World-class sales performers were twice as likely to collaborate across departments to pursue big deals. One key point of collaboration for enterprise deals was between sales and marketing. In this case, the world-class organizations were almost three times more likely to align the two groups than their rivals. When it came to retaining strategic accounts, the habit held, as the world-class organizations were twice as likely to manage them with interdepartmental teams and sales department members.

These top performing companies didn't team up for the sake of teamwork. "The purpose of collaboration is not collaboration itself. It's achieving better results in a shorter amount of time," said Miller Heiman research director Tamara Schenk. "It allows individuals with disparate areas of expertise and different roles to work together . . . to multiply their individual contributions."[5]

One of your most important leadership missions is to overcome the bias against cross-departmental collaboration. It's the only way you can become a world-class selling organization. With the dealstorming process, you can build a wide web but still maintain ownership of the process.

Why don't more sales leaders routinely gather up teams to attack their toughest sales? It seems like it would only make sense to throw a bunch of people in a room so they can figure out how to make the deal happen. You know, like brainstorming! While it's true that the more minds you bring to a problem the merrier the conversation can become, bad things happen when they don't know where they are going.

As Mark Nelson, senior vice president of sales at custom computer chip maker Altera told me, "Without the right process, you get a mess."

Let me make an important point here: dealstorming is *not* synonymous with brainstorming, the no-holds-barred approach to problem solving conceived by ad agency mogul Alex Osborn in the early 1940s. It's very important to explain exactly what the difference is and why the highly structured dealstorming process is so important to your team's success.

Osborn was one of the original "Mad men," who saved his fledgling Manhattan ad agency from post-Depression-era bankruptcy by landing the Goodrich account through a brainstorming meeting with his staff. He was so inspired by the victory that he committed the rest of his career to scaling his discovery to every nook and cranny of the business world.

It was the right stuff for an ad agency, where prospects looked for never-been-done-before campaigns that would break through the noise and grab attention. If you've watched as many episodes of *Bewitched* as I have, you know that it takes magic to come up with a truly novel idea for an ad campaign.

Osborn introduced his agency's idea-generation technique in 1942 in his book *How to Think Up*, with two key assumptions: You need a lot of ideas to find a blockbuster, and "Creativity is so delicate a flower that praise tends to make it bloom, while discouragement often nips it in the bud."[6] The four resulting rules for brainstorming included: Go for quantity. Defer judgment. Encourage wild ideas. Build on others' ideas.

By the 1960s, brainstorming was seen as the go-to method of "coming up with a lot of ideas" for product development and project management. Companies, civic organizations, and even governments employed Osborn's process, calling brainstorming sessions when feeling a little stale or under fire to "think up something quickly."

In most cases, a random group of people was ushered into a room where a facilitator would lead a conversation about how to solve a problem or create a new approach to an old one. A few hours later, a laundry list of ideas was produced, to be analyzed later by management. I'm sure you've been roped into a few of these brainstorming sessions. I know I have.

Over the last fifty years, mounting evidence suggests that, in many cases, Osborn's brainstorming technique doesn't always produce quality results. Yale University initially compared brainstorming groups with individuals working on their own and found that the latter outperformed the former in many cases.[7] Later studies explained why: incubation of a problem space is required to spark useful creations. Dominant personalities can take over a brainstorming meeting, causing everyone to anchor around their ideas—many of which aren't new. Instead of producing lots of ideas, participants are actually blocked in their ability to contribute as a result of filibustering. In some cases, thinking their ideas aren't required, participants dial out, a phenomenon known as "social loafing."[8]

In 2003, a widely cited study[9] by UC Berkeley researcher Charlan Nemeth challenged the key assumption of brainstorming: Does criticism decrease creativity? In this social science experiment, three groups were compared: those with no instructions for their brainstorming session, those with instructions not to critique ideas, and those with instructions to critique ideas thoroughly. Surprisingly, the third group, which debated ideas in session, produced by far the most useful ideas.

Still, there are situations in which Osborn's go-for-it approach is still valuable, such as product breakthroughs to revitalize a company or marketing ideas to differentiate a product in a dense marketplace. But in the case of business-to-business sales, a new process is required that encourages premeeting work, information sharing, candor, quality ideas, and results that are scalable and repeatable.

When you build a team to pursue a deal, its participants are expected to give their time and attention to it, in many cases forsaking their day-to-day functions. You don't want to waste it in an attempt to boil the ocean. You aren't looking for a "moon shot" idea as much as you are looking for a cascade of solutions over time. A deal team isn't looking for a list of possibilities but, instead, a winning play that takes them all to the next level.

To really excel with dealstorming, you need to build a team around high-value sales opportunities while at the same time managing the human dynamics that will ensue. Several sales leaders have shared stories with me about collaborative victories. To a person, they all wished they had a codified process in place that could repeat them at will.

"We've been pretty good at building teams when we have to," one prominent software executive told me, "but we need to make the leap to great, and that will require a process that everyone understands and buys in to." His point was that although smart and creative people know to fan out, curate the best ideas, and lead their ad hoc team, without a defined path, the game is unpredictable without a repeatable and scalable process.

You have no choice but to organize. Your prospects and best customers have already teamed up and, in some cases, brought in outside firepower to win the day. In many cases, you are outnumbered. They've built wide teams and continually improved their buying process and prepurchase knowledge.

With the dealstorming method we're about to dig deep into, you can fight fire with fire, organizing your own teams to compete for the win, and do so again and again.

THE DEALSTORMING METHOD

CHAPTER 4

Spinning Up a Solutions Web

For over twenty years, Ed Catmull pursued his dream of producing the first full-length motion picture by computer. It was a personal passion for him as well as a game changer for Pixar, a company founded to provide animation software for the next generation of films.

In January 1993, Pixar's vice president of creative development, John Lasseter, traveled to Burbank to pitch an idea for such a film to their distribution partners at Disney. After describing the story, about a boy and his toys—told from the toys' point of view—the project was given the green light and went into production.

A few months into the process, they faced their first big challenge.

According to Disney executive Jeffrey Katzenberg, the main character, Woody, needed to be less perky and more edgy. Lasseter responded by changing the script so Woody would display jealousy and, in one scene, throw Buzz Lightyear out the window. According to Catmull, Woody's character became "wholly unappealing." In late November, when Lasseter unveiled mock-up scenes of the movie on what Pixar insiders refer to as Black Friday, Disney shut down the production until a viable script could be written. In their eyes, Lasseter's response created more worries than solutions.

It was only the first problem that Lasseter and his staff needed to overcome on their journey to the silver screen.

Several months later, after the script was deemed viable, technology problems plagued the group as they attempted to ensure that the animated characters would display human qualities. To this point, Lasseter had been working with a vertical production team of writers, animators, and editors. But the level of skill and knowledge needed to build programs that would truly render Woody and the gang as lifelike, to animate them as cartoons had never before been animated, required a new type of team.

Lasseter and Catmull realized they needed to blow up their previous understanding of the kind of team they would need to solve a thousand problems. In *Creativity, Inc.*, Catmull wrote, "Getting the team right is the necessary precursor to getting the ideas right. Give a good idea to a mediocre team, and they will screw it up. Give a mediocre idea to a great team, and they will either fix it or come up with something better."[1]

The *Toy Story* challenge called for marshaling a previously unheard of level of human resources to make a film. It would showcase Pixar's software technology as well as ushering in a new era for the company as a movie maker. Steve Jobs, the company's top investor and board member, raised the stakes even higher by suggesting that an initial public offering closely follow the debut of the film.

So Lasseter went in on forming a multidisciplinary team that included computer scientists, puppet masters, clay artists, stop-motion animators, and a wide variety of technical directors, in addition to business leads (including Catmull) and a handful of other leaders at Pixar with expertise ranging from finance to operations to marketing. Lasseter thoughtfully selected his team members based on who had a stake in the outcome or who could bring problem-solving perspectives to the table. They were thoroughly briefed on the story background, technology challenges, and inputs from their partners at Disney. Their meeting space was designed to foster collaboration and a sense of meritocracy.

Painstakingly, the team hacked their way through a maze of challenges, bringing the movie to market on Thanksgiving Day, 1995. It grossed almost four hundred million dollars, fueled a successful IPO, and changed the course of Pixar. While much of their success was due to the team's creativity and relentless execution, without a proper project setup, Pixar likely would have failed. The success of the project truly depended on how well the team was organized and prepared.

The similarities between making a movie and landing a big deal or saving a key account are striking. Lasseter's team faced multiple decision makers, navigated layers of complex technology, dealt with Hollywood politics, and had to stand out in a dense market to succeed. Sound familiar? This team-based problem-solving approach, which would later be termed "the Brain Trust," worked again when Pixar made *Toy Story 2* and *Toy Story 3* as well as other groundbreaking movie projects they've taken on over time. Over the last decade, this team-based approach to problem solving has influenced my thinking greatly—and the formation of the Brain Trust and identification of the challenge share many similarities to the dealstorming stages of qualify and organize.

Dealstorming is a repeatable process that brings a collection of minds together around a sales challenge to move it forward. It leverages the insights, intelligence, and imagination of a diverse group of people who are aligned around the shared vision of getting to the next level of the sale.

The setup of the 'storm is the key to its success. In many of my interviews, I found that where there was an organic dealstorming tendency, the team-organizing stage left the most room for improvement. Too often, we think that the key to collaboration is in how we manage the groups as they convene. In fact, there are many avoidable hazards that come up in arranging and organizing the group prior to the meeting.

As I developed the dealstorming process at Yahoo! and then later for my consulting clients, I realized how difficult the setup stage could be. In some cases, we overresourced or underresourced the group. In others, the team selection process broke down. In several situations, team members arrived empty-minded, leading to long meetings that produced few good ideas.

To improve the premeeting process, I've consulted with colleagues with expertise on brainstorming, collaboration, knowledge management, and recruiting to figure out the best way to assemble a team and start the process off on the right foot.

Qualify

Think of what creates a storm in nature: hot air and cold air colliding. Because hot air is less dense, it's forced to rise over the colder air, triggering the storm cycle. In the case of a sales challenge, we can think of our selling efforts as hot air (no insult intended) and the buyer's efforts as cold air. When our best efforts are met with strong resistance, the sales process isn't working, and it's time to consider a dealstorm.

For sales leaders, this realization often occurs during the deal pipeline review process with reps. Most of my dealstorm consulting engagements were triggered this way. The leader determined that the system had been correctly applied, that the deal was stuck or the relationship was at risk, and that sales department resources were unlikely to move the situation forward. When a major account is in danger, the sales leader may determine that its significance immediately warrants cross-department collaboration—and then often recognizes that there is no effective sales process in place to save or resurrect it.

For account executives, the dealstorm trigger is usually the failure of a specific sales tactic and the realization that the deal is moving backward or taking an inordinate amount of time to advance. In some situations, it's a sudden cutoff of communications with the prospect or customer. In that event, the account executive consults with her manager about the situation to gain approval for dealstorming resources, including recruiting help from outside the sales department. This was how most of the dealstorms at Yahoo! started, although as time went by, some account executives were experienced enough with the process to contact ValueLab directly with their requests. Even then, we usually qualified the opportunity and looped in their managers prior to spinning up the 'storm.

Sales leaders: make sure everyone on your sales team is aware of dealstorming as a problem-solving tool for big sales challenges and understands what process needs to be followed to create one. Some of the most successful dealstorm projects I've been involved in came from the edges of a sales group far away from headquarters, where the war stories of sales success are shared by word of mouth. When I've rolled this out across companies, sales leaders have hosted seminars where the concept and process were explained fully. This book offers you an alternative dealstorming orientation tool that can be shared widely with all account executives and support staff, regardless of their location.

A dealstorm often requires significant resources from the account executive, her manager, and all the people who are recruited to participate in the process. Without a qualification stage, you can easily waste a lot of valuable people's time and effort chasing the wrong opportunities.

According to UC Berkeley management professor Morten Hansen, "People should launch a collaboration project only if the net value of collaboration is greater than the return minus both opportunity costs and collaboration costs."[2] He documented this point with a study he conducted involving Sterling, an information technology consulting firm that helps companies implement complicated enterprise resource planning (ERP) systems. Deals could earn up to fifty million dollars in fees per project. He noticed that some teams, when preparing SAP implementation bids to impress their prospect, would invest lots of time meeting with SAP experts inside Sterling to get their advice on perfecting the bid. Other teams would prepare the bid on their own.

When he analyzed sales performance over 182 projects, he discovered that the teams that prepared bids *without* collaborating with inside SAP experts won more projects. This astounded Hansen, so he dug into the details, only to find that the sales system in place was more than adequate at training account executives on all things SAP. The teams that collaborated for window dressing wasted valuable time that they could have invested in tailoring the project to the real needs of the prospect. It's a unique case study, for sure, but worth noting.

Conducting a dealstorm can be a time-consuming process. You need to schedule, prepare, and then conduct meetings; establish rapport with team members who haven't worked with you or others in the group; follow up with phone calls and write-ups; and then be willing to reciprocate when asked to repay the favor. That's why I've always spent a good portion of time qualifying the need for dealstorm team formation, based on known problems that are specific to a particular sales situation. In my consulting experience, over half the time the existing sales system was more than adequate for the account executive and her manager to solve the sales challenge at hand.

For sales leaders, the first check point for qualifying and staffing dealstorms is to verify that there really is a problem—a situation that cannot be changed without outside assistance—which requires collaboration. In typical deal-review format, identify which level the account executive feels stuck in, and what tactics were employed. Are you sure that the entire sales process was applied correctly?

For example, if a key account is in danger, review the escalation process already in place for account management, billing reconciliation, make-goods, or executive involvement. If a key prospect isn't responding to contact attempts, review the approach to ensure all avenues were taken. If a decision maker is pushing back on the value proposition, price, or product selection, review the applied sales collateral to make sure they are either up to date or correctly being used in this situation.

Once it's verified that it's a sales challenge to the system, not just for the particular account executive, it's time to calculate the level of resources you will need to commit to solving it. The following qualification formula is based on two variables: strategic value and degree of difficulty.

Value × Difficulty = Resources

The strategic value of a sales opportunity can be calculated in terms of revenue opportunity, branding power, or market penetration, taking into account the likelihood that your company's capabilities will add value over time.

You likely have a good handle on the threshold of revenue significance from an enterprise point of view; maybe it's a million dollars, or for smaller organizations, a few hundred thousand dollars. Take into consideration (echo) the account executive's and sales manager's definitions of significant as well. Sometimes, having resources to help them close what they perceive as a significant deal can give a boost to morale or even act as a hook for retention.

The branding power of a sale is best calculated by asking these questions: What would the key trade journals or bloggers say about my company winning or losing this account? What does it mean to the credibility of the service promise I am promoting to customers and prospects?

Brands are built around four key attributes: differentiation, relevance, esteem, and awareness. Ask yourself: "Does this potential deal drive my company's differentiation from the competition, and in other cases could it signal its market relevance or esteem?" Be careful, though, because without any research, almost any sales opportunity could be viewed as a brand booster. If in doubt, make contact with your marketing or research team to verify the brand opportunity.

Market penetration is achieved when you land a key prospect, signaling to its competitors and partners that your company is a player in the space. In the case of Neil Miklusak at LinkedIn (who was introduced in Chapter 1), landing a big advertising account with a prominent financial services firm could create a tipping point for social media marketing to be considered viable and appropriate in this heavily regulated and risk-averse industry.

At office leasing company Regus, landing a big enterprise deal for outsourcing entire corporate campuses would signal that they are no longer just in the small business space. Sande Golgart, the company's senior vice president of corporate accounts, referred to a prospective deal for an innovation incubator for large companies in the Silicon Valley as a "'trophy case study' that will finally make us relevant in the boardrooms of the Fortune 500." A single sale could produce a beachhead for his Regus sales team to make progress in the lucrative enterprise market.

Regardless of why you think the opportunity has strategic value, it's critical to look at it through the filter of your company's ability to deliver value to the customer. Otherwise, any big company with deep pockets or a high profile would score highly on this metric. Examine what capabilities or products you have that in all likelihood would be a fit for this prospect. See if there are relevant success or failure stories that can assist your judgment. It's still a guess at this point without more discovery work, but still, it's important to take into account.

This is critical for a few reasons. First, if you don't have confidence you can add value, it's hard to lead a dealstorm to victory. There is no purpose where there is no product–customer fit. Besides, in situations

where enterprise customers aren't happy with your service, the anticipated revenue is not usually recognized or make-good efforts clobber
profitability. Second, if you close the deal, then fail to deliver on your
promise, there is no branding or market penetration value.

Once you've assessed the strategic value of solving the sales challenge, give it a score from 1 to 10, with 10 being the highest value. This
is the first half of your qualification formula. If it's a 9 or a 10, at the
very least you may choose to escalate the involvement, even if it's relatively simple to solve with the right person and doesn't require collaboration. At Skillsoft, knowing the deal value helps Tom Cunningham
determine whether to brief his COO or involve the chief strategist.
(Note: Later, I'll talk about whether such escalation is a good idea in
a full-blown dealstorm.)

Next, we assess the degree of difficulty in solving the sales challenge, in light of the current sales methodology and assets available to
the account executive. We experience difficulty when faced with high
levels of resistance to our sales process and selling tactics. For example,
if the current sticking point is lack of trust by the prospect, this is an
emotional issue that is not easily solved; therefore, the level of sales difficulty is high. If the challenge is contacting and convincing multiple
decision makers and influencers, all with separate agendas, the degree
of difficulty is likewise high. On the other hand, if it's merely a matter
of opening a door at the prospect or getting a single person on the
phone, then the above-mentioned executive escalation process may do
the trick, thus saving a lot of time for everyone potentially involved.

Another way to think about the degree of difficulty is to assess how
many levels of the sale would present particularly difficult challenges.
For example, when advertising solutions provider Videology pursued
a mega services deal with Comcast, sales vice president Brett Tabano
knew up front that they would face a stiff challenge in locating all the
influencers in their bureaucracy, crafting a relevant selling proposition

in terms they could accept, and swaying Comcast executives to recognize Videology's strategic value and not just think of them as an "advertising network" that aggregated spot inventory. That's three levels of extreme pain.

Once you've identified the complexity you'll face, score the degree of difficulty, using the same 1 to 10 scale as you did for the strategic value of the opportunity.

Dealstorms come in all sizes, and resources dedicated to them should vary based on the cumulative score you've given the opportunity. The dealstorming process can also apply to the lowest value/difficulty situations, but it shouldn't require a budget or trigger involvement outside of the immediate sales group (rep, manager, support staff). For example, a low score (3/3) could signal a transactional opportunity with a single, medium-difficulty sticking point. That would qualify for a duo or trio storm, often between the account executive, sales manager, and perhaps an account manager. A 6/4 could necessitate bringing in a few more people from relevant groups. A 9/9 should trigger a wide dealstorm, possibly including outsiders from the partner value chain or even from the prospect or customer side of the table.

Once you've calculated the value and difficulty of the sales challenge, you can use the following table as a rough guide for resource allocation:

RESOURCE SCORE	BUDGET	TOTAL TEAM SIZE
70–99	Large	10–12
50–69	Medium	6–9
30–49	Small	4–5
10–29	No Capital	2–3
Example: Value = 8	Difficulty = 9	Resource Score = 72

A few clarifications on this table: budget refers to required capital for travel, lodging, meeting supplies, room rental, food, third-party research, etc. The total team size represents the number of people that are brought into a dealstorm as meeting participants at some point of the process. In my experience, a dealstorm's active team size scales up and down during the process because certain levels, such as convince, require more creative collaboration, whereas other levels, such as contract, can be solved with a few people.

Here's an illustration of how your team may come together, assuming you face challenges at every level of the sale:

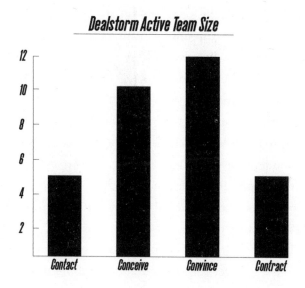

Dealstorm Active Team Size

For the largest or most complex deals, where there are multiple sticking points, you may decide, like Eric Gilpin did at CareerBuilder, to involve more than a dozen people on the working team. But modern research on team sizing by Rich Karlgaard and Michael Malone suggests that "the average team size is usually one fewer person than what the managers think they need."[3] The more you add, the more emotions, personalities, and opinions there are to manage.

There's an art and science to qualification. You might be more responsive to high strategic value, thus letting that be heavily weighted in your resource decisions. You might be a startup business unit or under pressure to cover off your market, making you more responsive to high-difficulty situations, even at a lower strategic value, say 3/8. After you and your team have conducted a few dealstorms, the true costs will manifest themselves and, over time, you'll figure out exactly how to employ this formula to maximize everyone's time and efforts.

Organize

Now that the value/challenge of the situation qualifies its resources, it's time to organize an appropriate team around it. The guiding concept here is to include all the necessary internal stakeholders so that problem solving and execution go hand in hand. Your stakeholders could be individuals affected by the financial outcome, the sales process, or resulting delivery requirements. They could be influencers, decision makers, or resource allocators in finance or operations. Whoever they are, they should possess insights, expertise, or relevant experience that could come into play in the dealstorm cycle.

It's important to keep in mind that in many cases the sales challenge will not qualify for a cast of dozens. Anyway, that would make meetings hard to manage. The more participants in each one, the more idea flow can get interrupted and the more difficult it is for everyone to participate. Additionally, thinking from an enterprise perspective, each meeting attendee is being taken off her job to attend, so there's a cost to each person's participation. To keep your team's size manageable, while you should be open to one-off conversations with a large group of people, you should be judicious about those who are formally a part of the team and included in all meetings and correspondence. To that end, try to recruit individual representatives from stakeholder groups. In my experience, the maximum number of people you should invite to any meeting is twelve, and that's only for high-resource-score challenges.

Dealstorm teams may scale up and down during a long sales cycle. That's why I make the distinction between the total team size and the active team size. During the contact level, teams can be as small as three or four participants. The Prudential Retirement large sales team swells during the conceive and convince levels, then usually pares down to just a few participants in the contract level. At Videology, the team size remains relatively constant, working on the deal collectively from end to end. Once a member has participated in a meeting, he likely will become invested in the outcome. So even though attendance at some meetings may not be required, team members are still on the team and should be kept in the loop on email updates. In several of my dealstorms, team members have contributed valuable insights between meetings, even though they hadn't attended the last meeting.

It's important to note that although everyone in the dealstorm has a voice in the discussion, not everyone necessarily has a vote in the process. This is not a democratic committee; the account executive owns the strategy, in consultation with her manager.

There are four roles in the dealstorm: problem owner, sponsor, resources,* and information master. It's critical that each person know their role; otherwise, meetings can descend into anarchy.

The problem owner is typically the person ultimately responsible for solving the sales challenge. This is usually the account executive or business development lead. He will ultimately recruit the team, create premeeting prep documents, run the meetings or conference calls, sift

---

*I chose "resources" as the label for this role as opposed to "team members" because it signifies that these participants are to bring their resourcefulness to the dealstorm. This term emphasizes the dealstorm team's reliance on their creative thinking and willingness to work on deliverables later.

through the insights and information, and determine next steps in consultation with his manager.

In rare situations, such as a sales challenge where the strategic value is a 10, the sales manager or an executive may ultimately decide to own the problem. Too often, though, it's hard to take off one's management hat when objective facilitation is required. Besides, it's a great learning experience for the account executive to conduct the dealstorming process. Often it gives him a unique perspective leading to more of a global view about how sales fits into the company's operations.

The sponsor's role is to qualify the dealstorm and then later, give real-time guidance as to the feasibility of potential solutions from both a policy and resource standpoint. The sales manager or group manager is a good fit for this role, as she often has a strong sense of what can be done within policy or precedent. Additionally, the sponsor can provide historical insights as she usually is a veteran of the company. In some situations, the sponsor will assist with recruiting when it involves higher-ranking executives or potential team members who haven't worked with sales before.

However, it's critical that the sponsor not interfere with the problem owner's role of facilitating the discussion from icebreaker to action items. Constant meddling or second-guessing will zap his confidence and add noise to the conversation. There can only be one leader in a meeting.

Speaking of which, here's an unconventional idea to consider: don't invite senior executives to play the role of sponsor unless radical departure from normal business is required. Many sales leaders I interviewed told me that big sales opportunities for their companies triggered executive involvement, oftentimes that of the CEO. His or her presence, however, slowed down the process more than it moved it forward. And involving them often took a heap of time—CEOs and other top-level executives are super busy, which means that coordinating the meeting is a nightmare of RE: RE: RE: emails to nail down when she can make it, if the date isn't rescheduled due to "another pressing issue." You don't have the flexibility to wait two months to schedule your dealstorming meeting around the CEO's schedule, usually.

Assuming your meeting is quickly scheduled, there are then politics to grapple with. Cass Sunstein and Reid Hastie, authors of the highly informative book *Wiser: Getting Beyond Groupthink to Make Groups Smarter,* report that the presence of a senior executive in the room leads to "happy talk," where the status quo is cheerfully defended by lower-level participants. "Group members like to please their leaders, who will therefore not tell the group what it needs to know," Sunstein and Hastie wrote.[4] In a dealstorm, the key to progress is to get everyone in the room to reveal what they know so the group can move from common knowledge to breakthrough understandings.

In a few situations, my interviewees suggested that having the CEO sponsor the meeting was part of the solution. When I'd ask them to identify what she did that moved the needle, the answer was unanimous: "Picked up the phone and called the prospect/customer CEO directly to work it out." That's not collaboration, that's senior-level escalation. And it doesn't scale or lead to process improvements. While it's the most direct solution in some situations, especially in the contact phase, when doors are hard to open, it's not a go-to strategy for deal solving.

The next role in the dealstorming process to outline is that of the resource. This group will make up the bulk of the team. Resources can come from anywhere in the company. They bring insights, research, ideas, objections, and the willingness to participate in postmeeting deliverables. As you assemble your resources, think wide, as in building a web of resources around a problem space.

Innovation consultancy firm IDEO influenced my dealstorm-building approach at Yahoo!. IDEO's teams solved tough design challenges issued to them by demanding clients, leading to inventions including the Palm Pilot, liquid soap dispensers, and the computer mouse. Their secret sauce was a blend of expertise and diversity in their collaborative teams. "Collaboration works especially well," cofounders Tom and David Kelley wrote in their book *Creative Confidence*, "when members bring different backgrounds or perspectives to the team."[5]

A good first step in building a wide team, particularly in identifying resources, is to ask, "Who knows something about this problem?" If the deal's sticking point is price or terms, add someone from finance (pricing or revenue recognition) or someone from legal. If you are working on defining the win-win idea or devising a custom solution, researchers, account managers, engineers, and designers are good resources because this challenge falls in their area of expertise. In some situations, a fellow account executive has solved a similar sales challenge (either in the same industry or with the same sticking point) and would be an excellent addition to the team.

Don't be afraid to reach out too widely, either. As creativity expert David Burkus found, "The people who solve tough problems often come from the edge of a domain. They have enough knowledge to understand the problem but don't have a fixed method of thinking. Their unique perspective allows them to generate a diverse set of ideas and still have enough domain knowledge to evaluate which ideas have merit."[6] One way to recruit at the edges is to draw up a map of who touches an account, from concept to delivery to billing to analysis and so on. Look at the outside edges of this deal stakeholder map to find surprising but helpful candidates for your team.

Here's an example of this stakeholder map for a technology solutions sales team that's pursuing a customer relationship management (CRM) deal with retailer Target. The map includes the sales team to the north, the delivery team to the south, the legal and operations team to the west, and the finance team to the east.

Stakeholder Map

Another way to identify resource candidates is to ask: "Who is usually excluded from these conversations for the wrong reasons?" In many cases, you'll identify people working in what one Microsoft sales leader termed "our land of no." These are the internal influencers who manage price, operations, risk, branding, and other parts of the company to ensure it runs smoothly to scale. It's easy for an account manager to see these people as blockers instead of colleagues with a job to do. But the fact remains that they are truly stakeholders in your situation. They often possess inside information about your company's operations and systems that may lead to a breakthrough in sales strategy. When you leave them out purposely, you are making the decision to proceed with blinders on.

Another approach is to seek out mirrors to the influencers or departments you are trying to sell to. Someone from IT might give you great insights on selling to technology decision makers. Someone from HR might help you sell a staffing or benefits administration solution. At Firehost, a managed cloud computing provider, sales leader Jim Hilbert organizes around matching titles. "If your influencer is a chief information security officer," he told me, "you bring in your CISO or someone who used to be one because he knows the same language and understands the world your influencer lives in. It's like having a Vulcan mind meld."

When you include them in a dealstorm, they not only contribute, they become part of the team. Mark Schmitz, COO at SAP Cloud, told me why he confers with nonsales functions for this reason: "When we partner on deals with leads in revenue recognition in finance, they become consultative partners with the sales force and not just the police!"

Here's a final note on the resource candidate identification process: add someone who is helpful to the team but not financially or politically tethered to its success. He or she might have deep knowledge of the customer, the industry, or your product but will not gain or lose personally based on the outcome. Abe Smith, a former tech executive at Webex (and now at Oracle) tells me, "Sometimes, you need to involve an expert with no stake in the outcome. Her lack of connection to the deal might make for advice more pure and forthcoming. She will not be subject to any false constraints that insiders often have in these problem-solving sessions. She won't know what she doesn't know."

As a last check-off, confer with your sponsor or early-stage team members and ask: "Who's missing? Whom could we invite that would bring some unique value to the table?" In many situations, you'll get a surprising nomination from the edges of your enterprise. In some cases, this exercise leads to adding someone at the last minute who will play a vital role in the project.

The last role in the dealstorm meeting is the information master. In larger opportunities, this person is in charge of organizing, recording, distilling, updating, and distributing the information related to the meetings. In smaller dealstorms, he is on point only during meetings, jotting down the ideas on flip charts, then, later, turning them over to the problem owner for follow-up.

Because information drives the process, the information master is a critical role to fill. This was a key lesson for Brett Tabano, from video advertising platform Videology, who told me, "For large projects, the information organizer is one of the most important roles in the process because he or she compiles the memory of your team, which determines the quality of its execution."

In my experience, the most effective information masters come from groups charged with creating documents for diverse audiences: marketing, sales enablement, and training. This, too, was Brett Tabano's experience. He said, "Throughout the dealstorming process, you are gathering information from a multitude of voices and perspectives. Having someone who can organize it all into a single voice, from project reports to postmortems, is the secret to the team's success."

If possible, the information master should create a shared workspace where anyone on the team can contribute information, suggest edits, or provide updates to ensure highly dynamic and accurate information flow. This can be done by sharing documents or presentation collateral via tools such as Google Docs, Evernote, Dropbox, and the like. I don't suggest sales force automation platforms here, as many of your dealstorm team members aren't in the department and don't have access to it.

A meeting-only information master can be recruited from one of the resources at the beginning of the meeting. They will be in charge of filling up flip charts, whiteboards, or projected computers with ideas, issues, and action items brought up in the meeting.

A caveat: the problem owner shouldn't attempt to play information master during meetings, as he needs to maintain focus on gathering insights, helping the group converge on the next play, and gathering commitments for execution.

Now that you have a bead on your potential team members, it's time for the problem owner to recruit these people to join the dealstorm. There are no shortcuts here, sales executives and leaders. You're not imposing a draft; you must build an all-volunteer force. In order to drum up innovation in your sales process, you're going to need opt-in from your troops. DePaul University professor Lisa Gundry and Lucent executive Laurie LaMantia documented this in their study of the formation of breakthrough teams. "Creative energy is lost in the feeling of choicelessness. But when we want to do something, it's not a chore."[7]

As you prepare your invitation to the dealstorm, to quote leadership expert Simon Sinek, "Start with *why*." Sure, you've already determined the value of the deal earlier, but oftentimes it's sales-centric and won't resonate outside of your departmental silo. As one sales collaboration veteran explained to me, "The key is for all the participants to understand the strategic nature of the deal in terms they care about. When you focus only on monetary value, only certain people respond. Technology and operations don't care about it like sales does, and they might think that working on their normal job projects is a better way to succeed."

Make sure your *why* arguments speak to a purpose that will resonate widely throughout your organization. Sande Golgart at Regus positioned the importance of "being relevant in the boardroom" to support his enterprise sales team's value proposition. If Regus makes the leap from small business to Fortune 5000 leasing, the company's customer base is more attractive to financial analysts who calculate the all-important price-to-earnings ratio that drives stock value. For fellow shareholder employees who care about their portfolios, that can be a good hook for contributing to the dealstorm.

While "carrot and stick" is one way to motivate, be careful because this tactic is employed routinely by senior executives for all forms of change management and belt tightening. Outside market factors could dilute the power of any single sales opportunity or account save to really move the needle, especially in the eyes of the brightest people at your company.

At Yahoo!, I learned the value of leveraging market culture, where there's an intense focus on beating the competitor. When we'd get stuck on a big deal with a major advertiser, oftentimes we'd find ourselves in a runoff against our archrival, AOL, led by their executive sponsor, Ted Turner. When I'd approach engineers, financial analysts, researchers, and the like to join our dealstorm, I'd use our rivalry with AOL as a lever to get them emotionally invested in our success. Our goal was to beat them, pure and simple. This drove dealstorm recruiting and instilled the tendency to collaborate instead of compete. After all, there is a constant scrum at most companies for technical, financial, and political resources. As professor Morten Hansen advises when creating a collaboration project, "The goal must put competition on the outside!"

Using this approach creates a sense of unity, which is important when you need to get team members to build on each other's ideas, especially when they don't normally work together.

With a strong *why* in hand, you need to individually pitch candidates to join your dealstorm. Do not attempt to send out a single email to the entire list of candidates and expect to get any uptake. Mass emails often languish in our inbox, or when opened, come off impersonally. If someone is important enough to invite to your project and give you his spare time, he is worth a customized invitation.

Personally, I prefer a phone call or a face-to-face pitch, as these are much more effective at conveying your intentions and passion for the project. Lead with the *why* and then be specific as to why you see her as an asset to the group. Don't ask her to attend a meeting. Instead, invite her to join the team. There's more to it than hanging out for an hour in a conference room, and besides, going to another meeting sounds like torture, not adventure.

If you use email to recruit your dealstorm team, make sure to customize each one. Include the *why* behind the 'storm, what he adds to the team, and the resources you are asking him to bring to the table (insights, information, innovations, etc.). According to consultant Robert Hargrove (*Mastering the Art of Collaboration*), "Design invitations to collaborative meetings that excite and reassure people"—let them know that their time won't be wasted and that their voice will be heard.[8]

One of my consulting clients used video invitations to pull together teams, conveying her passion for solving the challenge as well as her admission that, in the past, company-wide projects like this too often failed to use every person around the table. (For video email resources, visit TimSanders.com/DealStorming.) Another client assured potential team members in his invitation that they would have time to present their ideas and that good ones would be championed and then later recognized during the "victory parade." He even embedded a graphic of a New England Patriots post–Super Bowl parade, as the company was based in Boston, and he knew it would evoke an emotional response.

Once someone agrees to join your team, confirm his participation by email or, better yet, send him a written note, card, or gift as a way of saying "Welcome to our world!" One of my consulting clients in the software industry creates a document that looks like a movie poster, where the "cast" for the dealstorm is listed. It's posted on the company intranet as well as hung in hallways to generate enthusiasm for the coming dealstorm. Here's an example of what one could look like.

(Download the movie poster template at TimSanders.com/Dealstorming)

I bet this sounds like a lot of work so far, right? Well, strap yourself in, because it's just the beginning of the process. I won't kid you: it gets harder, especially for the problem owner. In the next chapter, you'll learn how to set up your newly created team for victory—even before they convene for the first time.

CHAPTER 5

Chance Favors the Prepared Mind

J ust a few months after I arrived at Yahoo!, Tom Peters and Julie Anixter invited me to participate in the Crave Conference in San Francisco, which focused on design-centered innovations. At the event, I spent time with their partner in creativity, Tom Kelley, cofounder of IDEO.

My ValueLab at Yahoo! was just coming together. We were being called into strategic sales and partnership opportunities to present, brainstorm, and, increasingly, facilitate cross-departmental meetings.

"When a pack of Yahoos come together around a problem," I told Tom, "it gives us a much better chance of solving it." I went on to explain that each solutions meeting was like buying a lottery ticket—except that our odds were much better.

Tom smiled at me and then quoted Louis Pasteur, "Chance favors the prepared mind."

He went on to explain how IDEO's design solution meetings were the culmination of layers of preparation, starting with research, which led to the creation of a design brief that detailed requirements, background, and resources for premeeting consumption. These briefs gave each attendee food for creative thought, enabling them to show up for meetings with ideas in hand to discuss with the group.

His advice had a profound impact on my perspective, reminding me of a quote attributed to Abraham Lincoln: "If I had six hours to chop down a tree, I'd spend the first four sharpening my axe." Until then, I had followed the same misguided notion of countless brainstorm organizers: have participants show up empty-handed, brief them quickly, and then spend the remaining time coming up with and vetting any and all ideas that might arise about the challenge at hand.

Moving forward, days prior to any ValueLab-led meeting, we'd prepare our participants thoroughly. My team and I would collect information from account executives, coordinators, and business development leads on the opportunity, the playing field, and proposals to date. We'd then do our own research on the prospect company as well as their executives and the contacts we were working with. Then, to avoid overwhelming our Yahoos with too much information, we boiled down the essential material into a short document we referred to as the parse.

The solutions meetings we organized and hosted were much more effective with the presence of the parse. The parse (which later became the deal brief) was appended by participants as the project went along and served as an orientation tool for people joining the deal team. Later, when we presented solutions to prospects, our assumptions were much more accurate, moving them to agreement much more quickly.

By doing our homework, we enabled our deal teams to be highly creative and productive from the get-go.

When I've asked sales leaders about meetings gone wrong, they often attribute failure to a lack of preparation. On the other hand, when I've witnessed breakthrough meetings, it was because everyone showed up briefed, excited, and armed with ideas and/or good questions.

The key to preparing for a dealstorm is to create a compact but comprehensive deal brief. It's a sales-centric modification of design briefs from innovation circles. "Great briefs are the basis of the team's work," says Unilever marketing executive Diggi Thompson. "They set up the task and what you hope to accomplish. Good briefs are clear, single-minded, short, and inspiring. They should harness the brain's grappling hooks."[1]

As problem owner, it's your job to prepare this brief in consultation with the information master on larger opportunities. Try to limit it to four pages so that it's not an intimidating read. In some cases, it can be informed by elements from the request for proposals (RFP) submitted by the prospect or existing client. As brand consultant Ralph Ardill testified, "A lot of breakthrough work comes through a brief that might be given to us by a client, that we've deconstructed to get to the real problem."[2]

You *must* send the deal brief to your resources at least three days prior to a dealstorm, and if possible, allow them a weekend to review the brief before participating in the meeting. Creativity expert Keith Sawyer studies the science of human innovation and believes that this incubation period is likely the most important part of the problem-solving or solution-finding process. "Creativity requires that we encounter and internalize previous parts of insight, and it requires incubation time for those parts to combine in the mind," he writes. "During incubation, existing ideas bounce into each other, almost like atoms in a chemical soup."[3] Unlike Google's search engine or an ultrafast computer processor, our mind doesn't make all the necessary connections right away, which is why it's important to give everyone on the team some time to read and sit with the deal brief before the meeting.

The deal brief should be written to guide your resources through the problem, the ultimate opportunity, project goals, players, history, and current situation. It should follow this format:

- ➤ Problem Question
- ➤ Opportunity and Goal Statement
- ➤ Influence Map
- ➤ Account/Prospect History
- ➤ Recent Developments
- ➤ Constraints and Resources
- ➤ Premeeting Assignment

The reason I choose a problem question, rather than a problem statement, is that it's more open ended. In *The Innovative Sale*, creative sales expert Mark Donnolo declares, "Questions are more powerful than statements. They are the fuel for divergent thinking."[4] Open-ended questions posit that possibilities exist. Statements can have the opposite effect, making the current obstacle seem insurmountable. However, coming up with a good question is harder than simply stating where you are stuck in the sales challenge solution process.

A good problem question identifies the exact sticking point and queries the reader to put their mind to work solving it. If you pose a vague problem question, such as, "How can we save this account?" or "How can we close this deal?" you aren't providing a good springboard for useful or relevant ideas. You are asking your reader to start from scratch.

Here's a situation I've seen in countless companies: you're dealing with a powerless champion at your prospect who won't introduce you to the real decision maker(s). You've gleaned a lot of good information from him or received some small orders, but it's clear that you will never complete a strategic deal unless you get face time with key influencers or decision makers. In many cases, a key influencer is your contact's boss, grand boss, or one of the corporate chiefs.

Because he's on your side, you don't want to alienate your champion by simply going over his head. Ask yourself, "If he thinks we would add value, why isn't he escalating this to those in power?" The first answer might be, "Because he doesn't think it would interest them." Now ask, "And why is that?" Your answer might be, "He doesn't see us as strategic to the company's success. In his view, we are just a transactional vendor."

Now we are getting to the real sticking point. In this case, the problem question would be, "How can we prove we are strategic enough to be introduced further up the corporate decision making chain?" This is a far more specific and thought-provoking problem question than the obvious, "How can we go around him without upsetting him or making him look bad?"

Another example: if you can't get past the conceive stage, where you need to create a custom solution that generates measureable value, start the question-finding process by asking "Why can't we progress?" until you find the root problem. The first answer might be, "Because we cannot see their back-end technology stack, so we can't make the proper calculations." Now ask, "Why is that?" With some research, you can get at the real problem, which could be that the prospect has policies that restrict any outsiders from seeing their trade secrets, which include their technology configuration. This reveals a potential problem question: "How might we convince the prospect to make an exception to policy and allow us to see their schematics?"

This exercise is based on the 5 Whys, a problem-finding technique pioneered by quality engineer Sakichi Toyoda at Toyota Motor

Corporation in the 1960s. With practice, you'll find that the "And why is that?" exercise is the secret to finding the right problem question. You'll be repeating this during your dealstorm meeting because your group may shine a better light on the root cause, which is critical to solving any sales challenge.

Next comes the opportunity statement, which should be concise, yet inspiring. First, for sales and management participants, reveal the revenue opportunity. Next, state the higher-purpose intangible opportunity, such as beating the competition, strengthening your market position, or in some cases, standing out as an agile company. This is essential for creating the shared vision, the glue that holds the entire team together.

The goal statement lays out exactly what dealstorm success will look like. It should contain exact steps—get a meeting with the CEO, make it to the finals of the RFP process, obtain a signed contract—as well as a time line for completion. Consult with your sponsor to come up with a reasonable goal date for the deal to be closed or the sales challenge to be resolved. This may be done through normal forecasting methods or by looking for a calendar date event, whether it's the end of the quarter, the prospect's budget closing date, etc.

The next section lays out the influence map, which is a critical part of the deal brief. It puts the problem question and opportunity in the context of the people who make up the buying team. In some cases, they are organized into a procurement circle or vendor management board (the analog to your dealstorm). Often, it's a loose confederation of influencers and decision makers who make up the buying web.

Each listing on the influence map should, whenever possible, provide a direct link to a bio or more information. If there's not one on their corporate website, LinkedIn can be an effective tool. You can look up common contacts, previous work, or educational experiences, and get a better understanding of what drives their thinking. (Note: Instruct everyone on the team to set his or her LinkedIn profile viewing settings to anonymous so in the event one of these contacts clicks on "Who's Viewed Your Profile," he doesn't see a list of people from your company. That could come across as a little creepy.)

Start to flesh out your influence map by listing current contacts and people you're already dealing with at the prospect, including their titles and whether they are decision makers, influencers, or information providers. If possible, list whom they report to in the organization. Next, list key influencers and decision makers you've identified but haven't yet engaged.

The last section of the influence map should include any known blockers, or what one technology sales leader refers to as "the bully with the juice." Often, these blockers appear in the deal brief in red type. They are the people who must be won over in order for you to make progress or ultimately solve the challenge. If you're in technology sales, your known blocker might be the chief information officer, who has a legacy relationship with one of your competitors or a disdain for any significant changes made by non-IT leads.

Aside from bio information, conduct a little search engine sleuthing to see if anyone on the influence map has been quoted talking about a topic that's relevant to the problem question or your company's value proposition. If you find a hit, include the link directly beneath her name.

The next section of the deal brief is a review of the account or prospecting history. Your sales force CRM platform can come in handy here. Organize this section along a time line, and keep it concise. Include what you've attempted, what information you provided, what the prospect's response was, and, whenever possible, a short quote from one of them to give context and color to the situation.

It's important to stress that transparency is absolutely required for any collaborative project to succeed. You cannot withhold any key facts from your team. In my consulting work, I've seen teams unravel when the truth came out about previously withheld information. Your honesty will garner trust, which is an essential ingredient for effective collaboration.

In the case of trying to save an account, you may very well have to fess up about mistakes you've made, or errors in judgment or execution by other associates. (Consult with your sponsor to determine the proper way to reveal these facts within the context of your company's politics and culture.)

In pursuing new business, don't leave out details regarding presentations gone wrong or misunderstandings you've had with the prospect contacts. While I'm not advocating being self-effacing, it's important that your entire team understand your role in the current sales challenge that necessitated a dealstorm.

In the event that the opportunity is first-time business, refer to the exact sales collateral presented or given to the client. Link to where it's posted online, either on your intranet or a cloud-based service (Box, Dropbox, Salesforce, etc.). Do not include elements such as slide decks or PDFs as attachments when you send the deal brief. You want to send a single document to the team, not thirty megabytes of stuff for them to wade through (and curse you for).

In the case of an account save or resurrection, you'll need to paint a clear picture of what happened. You can't possibly bring back the business if you aren't clear on why it went away in the first place. Like you did earlier with your problem question, you need to keep asking "And why is that?" until you get to the root cause of the breakup.

One of my consulting clients was trying to restore a million-dollar deal they'd lost to a competitor. This introspective exercise of asking "And why is that?" revealed that the client thought he was being over-charged for the service. The next iteration of "And why is that?"

revealed that their agreement was set up to provide a base number of service instances and then add-on charges for each one over the limit, at a higher price. Asking "Why did that lead to them feeling overcharged?" led to an important discovery: the client contact who signed the agreement and then paid the bill wasn't the same person who ordered the services. The two groups weren't comparing notes, so when the bill showed up, it was a disturbing surprise to everyone involved and generated the ill feelings that led to termination of the relationship.

You can imagine what an important deal brief detail this was for the entire dealstorm team. It gave them a solid starting point for problem solving. They were able to start with the communication disconnect and focus efforts on restoring trust instead of cutting price.

The next section lists recent developments in which you'll specifically itemize the findings or situation that triggered the need for a dealstorm. It could be the last meeting, where the prospect didn't buy in to your value proposition. It could be a competitor's action that led to the client cutting off or reducing business with your company. It could be an organizational change that altered the influence map, budget, or even the value proposition.

The key with the recent developments section is to be specific and not to convey any defensiveness. As the problem owner, you are likely on the front lines of this situation and, at times, the recent developments section can feel like a reflection on your performance or even your character. A mantra I always passed along to my dealstorming clients here is to objectify their selling failures as "business is just business."

Also list recent developments in the prospect's or client company's strategy, market position, competitive set, or other relevant topics that could influence your potential deal. Mergers, layoffs, new initiatives, executive moves, and such can provide a lot of food for thought for your upcoming meeting. To keep this section short, list the headline and then a link to the article with more information.

Now that you've oriented your team to the outside world of the deal, it's time to look internally at constraints and assets. Constraints include the limits you face as you look for solutions. Knowing your constraints is liberating because it defines the box you are expected to work within. You might be thinking, "Wait a minute, aren't we supposed to let our minds wander freely to truly be innovative?" This might seem to be the case, but actually this lack of boundaries makes it hard for us to productively focus on solutions.

Absent an awareness of constraints, many ideas offered up in dealstorms will be unworkable or downright silly, wasting our time and embarrassing those outside of the day-to-day mechanics of the sales process. By thinking inside the box, you limit the range of possibilities to those that you and your team can actually act upon right away.

In some cases, knowing constraints can lead to breakthroughs that may benefit your sales process. Columbia University professor Patricia Stokes heads up the university's Constraints, Variability & Creativity Lab. In her research, she has found that the presence of constraints drives creativity and has made possible many of the most innovative works of our time, including breakthroughs in art, advertising, and architecture.[5] For example, when Frank Lloyd Wright set out to produce buildings with organic forms, he was faced with a material constraint. Wood was the basis for construction at the time. It was plentiful, affordable, and easy to use. But it didn't lend itself to the round and natural shapes he conceived. Reinforced concrete was limited to floorings, as it was too heavy to use for entire structures. He creatively solved the weight problem by developing light but effective steel columns to support his creations. His innovation, found by working within a set of constraints, had a huge impact on modern architecture.[6]

Constraints are a function of your internal policies, regulations, industry norms, or the prospect's or client's norms and policies. At one financial services technology provider I work with, "No customization of our core software" is a constraint that needs to be respected. It's how they scale their business. At a defense contractor I counseled, the key constraint was "No selling below material costs plus 20%," which took discounting out of the solution arsenal. In some situations, the constraint can be external, such as, "The deal must be signed by the end of the year in order for us to honor the quote or level of services."

Constraints can include price, terms, window of opportunity, prospect or customer culture, contractual obligations, prospect or customer budget, regulatory and legal requirements, contact of record (e.g., agency or procurement), geographical limitations (too far away to visit face to face), and available products or services. Likely, with a little contemplation, you'll find even more.

Alongside constraints, your assets are also important to itemize, as they provide fertile ground for solution development. When I worked with internal sales clients at Yahoo!, our ValueLab team always asked the problem owners, "What do we have to work with?" as a starting point. You'd be surprised at how often they were so mired with the problem that they hadn't itemized which assets they could bring to bear (other than escalation to senior executives or our group).

Available assets could include services outside of the scope of your products, such as research, design work, creative consultation, financial analysis, or customer education. For example, at Cox Media, a client was ready to pull an account due to the perception that it wasn't working. Marketing's research team was brought in to analyze the ad agency's buys on their radio network and discovered that the ads were running on the wrong stations, against the wrong personalities, and in the wrong formats for the product that the client was marketing. This led to a new advertising placement strategy that produced dramatically better results. The client stayed with Cox and eventually doubled their book of business.

Your executives, spokespeople, and best clients are also assets that can potentially help you move your deal along or repair key relationships. At larger companies, another division may already have a relationship with your prospect, which can serve as reference or connector.

Lastly, your reputation is an asset that can help you, especially in the contact and convince levels. It can be documented via brand ratings, industry ratings and awards, or publications in trade journals or respected publications.

The final section of the deal brief is the premeeting assignment, which should be customized for each member of your team based on what you want him to research, prepare, or think about.

In certain situations, you may need to ask resources to do some additional work prior to the meeting to maximize the impact of the time the group spends together. You'll make this determination based on their capabilities, resources, or areas of expertise. You might ask one team member to provide more background on the influence map, for example, and another to develop potential solutions to the stated sticking point, such as an approach to contacting a key influencer at the prospect or a suggested combination of products and services to propose. You might ask a team member to do some research into a proposed solution you are considering. Whatever the task, keep it to a single request and avoid multiple, difficult assignments that will overwhelm.

In the event you don't have a premeeting assignment in mind for a particular recipient, leave this section off the deal brief.

The process of creating the deal brief will help you clarify and understand your sales challenge inside and out and, in some cases, avoid the need for a dealstorm altogether. The more you think about the totality of what surrounds the challenge, the more likely it is to trigger immediate insights and solutions.

I know the deal brief looks like a boatload of work—and, at the beginning, it is. But that's what is required to solve the toughest sales challenges. The more you create deal briefs, the quicker the process will become. You can download a deal brief document template at TimSanders.com/Dealstorming.

Before you send out your deal brief, make sure your sponsor has read it and agrees with your analysis of the present situation, recent developments, constraints, and assets. Once you hit the SEND button, it's off into the wild for better or for worse.

Send out the deal brief in individual emails. This avoids a reply-to-all free-for-all and also gives you the chance to personalize each note. This email should thank the recipient for being a part of the team and encourage him or her to read the deal brief and to respond with any suggested changes or questions. The email should also include the time and place of the meeting.

If possible, call all team members the day after you send the brief to ensure they have received it and to see if they have any questions. Even if they haven't read it yet, your phone call dramatically increases the chances that they will, which is critical to their successful participation in the coming 'storm. One of my consulting clients offers an Amazon or Apple gift certificate to the resource who exhibits the best understanding of the deal brief—their dealstorming sessions start with a game show–like quiz that measures participants' knowledge of the problem question, influence map, or prospect company developments. In cultures like this, such encouragement and gamification really motivate participants to read the brief and prepare notes on it.

There's another piece of prep work that the problem owner or the sponsor might need to do. For some dealstorms, you will invite people from groups across your company who historically don't cooperate easily. Likely they operate in hardened silos, where information is considered power, and, as a result, often withhold ideas or information from outside groups. In some cases, there is an ongoing dispute between two parties or groups you are mixing together in your collaborative web.

In these cases, a phone call with both parties or short meeting with all of them together is required to bring any hostility or chronic misunderstanding to the surface and hopefully neutralize it prior to the dealstorm. This is a key function of the sponsor: to deal with internal politics that can get in the way of solution making. I caution against trying to accomplish this in an email, which often fails to provide the nuances required for dealing with emotionally charged situations.

During such an advance, olive-branch call, it's important to start with the sales challenge that's on the table and what it means to the company and everyone involved. Be very transparent about who else is part of the deal team, including any frenemies to whom you are talking. It's important to acknowledge the conflict or misunderstanding and then ask if there's anything you can do to prevent it from spilling over into the meeting. Remember to thank him for participating, and assure him that it will make a big difference in finding the solution.

For the problem owner, there's a final piece of prep work: study your deal brief and give your mind an assignment to chew on it prior to the dealstorm. During your off time, casually consider the problem space and the contents of the brief while you do chores, play games, watch TV, take a walk, or whatever gives you the chance to passively think on the whole situation. Many of my best ideas have emerged while engaged in mindless but mindful activities. As potential breakthroughs come to you, write them down or throw them into a document (I use Evernote).

As I'll explain in the next chapter, the problem owner is usually the facilitator of the dealstorm, not the person who comes to the meeting with all the answers. These thoughts that come to you during your own incubation are your reserves, in case the group isn't forthcoming with potential solutions. Additionally, by vegging out on the problem space, you'll make connections that may well be validated during the dealstorm—and those are the ones that are likely to be valid solutions.

If anything, your extensive pre-dealstorm preparation will give you a strong sense of confidence in yourself, your team, and the project. When you put in all the hard work, your mind rewards you with ideas, positive feelings, and a sense that you deserve to win. Mark Cuban, with whom I used to work at Broadcast.com, was one of the folks who inspired me in my understanding of up-front work. He considers it the difference maker in life. On this subject, he often paraphrased one of his influential role models from his college days at Indiana University, basketball coach Bobby Knight: "Everybody has got the will to win. It is only those with the will to prepare that do win."

CHAPTER 6

Making Meetings Magic

I cut my teeth facilitating cross-company summits at Hughes Aircraft in the mid-'80s. There, I led quality circle meetings, which were part of a greater effort to reduce manufacturing defects through collaboration. Engineers, assembly line managers, quality-control specialists, vendor relationship supervisors, and personal development directors all came together to talk about how we could boost output and stem the rising tide of rework.

As a graduate student, I was quite young for the task, and I struggled mightily to maintain control over the deliberations, which often descended into arguments and finger pointing. They seemed more like corporate group therapy sessions than problem-solving exercises.

Tail between my legs, I huddled with my manager, who instructed me to conduct a "deep dive" on how to lead meetings, especially those with participants who didn't necessarily work well together. I studied how other companies succeeded in the same situation and came across research on how 3M (formerly known as Minnesota Mining & Manufacturing) mastered their meetings through design. 3M's leaders believed that strong communications between associates stemmed from transparency and mutual respect. They also understood that when diverse groups of people convened, magic could happen. They developed a meeting management team that injected art and science to the process.

I implemented my own version of 3M culture at Hughes with "Make Meetings Magic," a theme that reframed our quality efforts as an exercise in sharing information in order to empower everyone to succeed. I included this theme on the invitations I sent out as well as the posters I designed by hand, which hung in the hallways and meeting rooms.

When we came together, I explained to participants how Hughes had the potential to leapfrog the competition in terms of quality if we could bring our minds together. I revealed research from companies like 3M, Motorola, and Toyota, demonstrating the relationship between meeting effectiveness and productivity-driving collaboration. I challenged meeting attendees to "play to win" and focus on uncovering information and insights buried in some silo.

At first, my motivational introduction was met with bemused smiles and folded arms. With each meeting, I layered more supporting data, peppered with recent industry or news reports connecting the meeting at hand with the threats to our business I was talking about.

Over time, our meetings became increasingly productive and more fun. Under the premise that "anything can happen when we know everything," we compared notes across department lines, laughed, argued, debated, and most of all learned a lot about how our plant really operated.

I carried this experience into my role at Yahoo!'s ValueLab, where we were tasked with leading dealstorming meetings around the company. By then, the 3M Meeting Management Team had published its findings in *Mastering Meetings* (McGraw-Hill, 1994), which gave me even more food for thought, along with myriad facilitation guides from every corner of the globe.

"Whenever we convene," I would say to my dealstorm attendees, "there are great expectations, great opportunities, and great costs. Let's not just pass the time hoping we'll get something out of the confined exercise. Let's make some magic happen during our time together."

Over the next few years, I learned exactly what it took to lead a diverse group of minds to come together around a big sales challenge. And win.

The primary purpose of the dealstorm meeting is to improve the problem owner's information quality and give her additional ammunition to advance to the next level. The meeting's stretch goal is to set the next best play. The aspirational goal is to generate buy-in, especially among those who will deliver on the deal once won.

In many situations, the information revealed in the meeting leads the problem owner to find his solution right away. Too often, common knowledge (*what we all know*) is driving current efforts, which aren't working. The meeting leader needs to create a safe place where information flows, especially that which is only known by a few. In *Wiser*, Cass Sunstein and Reid Hastie point out, "When people from different offices and departments feel free to say what they know, group decisions get a lot better and big mistakes are avoided."

The next best play is the action that will be taken after the meeting to move the deal to the next level. This is something I took from Duke basketball coach Mike Krzyzewski, who focused his teams on the next play—not the past, and not even the bigger picture. By "best," I mean that the group has found a potential solution that is head and shoulders above the rest of the options discussed.

In a dealstorm, when you bring to the table everyone who has a stake in the deal, postdeal execution goes more smoothly. These stakeholders will deliver the services or products or conduct arbitrage such as billing, revenue recognition, or case study marketing. When their voices are part of the conversation at the beginning and not after the deal is signed, you'd be surprised how much enthusiasm they bring to the back end of the process. Involving them in the conversation produces a greater likelihood that when it comes time to deliver on the deal, they'll be at the ready to assist.

In most situations, the problem owner (aka the account executive) is up for the task and should serve as the meeting's facilitator. It is my personal bias that she should be given a chance, as it's a great leadership development experience. Additionally, when the deal is signed and in delivery mode, she will possess more social power to lead everyone to execute.

However, I've seen several situations where the account executive is either too timid or the stakes are too high for her facilitation skill set. In some situations, the group's mix is a disaster waiting to happen. Keith Murnighan, professor at Northwestern's Kellogg School of Management, observes, "When some teams diversify, they create a dangerous fault line . . . which sets the team up for an earthquake."[1]

I've seen this happen when a dealstorm team includes engineers, salespeople, and finance leads. The differences of role and personality must be managed with care because they don't take care of themselves. And when a clash erupts due to poor meeting leadership, there can be collateral damage to relationships, which could block future collaboration.

The sponsor (often the sales manager) should decide whether

someone besides the account executive should be brought in to serve as facilitator. You don't want cross-departmental meetings to be a waste of time or a pain to sit through—it will hurt your chances when you try to form future dealstorms.

The meeting facilitator must possess the following qualities:

Listening skills: He or she should be able to resist the urge to make statements during the process that inhibit participants from sharing information and ideas. After leading hundreds of collaborative meetings at the Palo Alto Research Center, John Seely Brown advises: "Active listening not only requires giving people the gift of your presence but also suspending your position and putting a tremendous amount of energy in understanding [the participant's] position."[2] This means that the facilitator should remain neutral to ideas and corporate ideologies, and let participants express themselves fully.

The facilitator needs to read the room as well. This involves looking for participants who, by their body language, demonstrate that they want to say something or are becoming agitated or disengaged. She should also note personality types as well, which could come in handy when creating small groups.

Protectiveness: When you gather up a diverse group of professionals, you must possess personal strength if you want to lead them to produce meeting value. A good facilitator protects the misfits, who are often shunned by others. Misfits often have nested information, which just may reveal the root cause of the problem or its solution. Too often, anything they say is colored by their personality and disregarded, even if they are right.

A strong facilitator also encourages the most junior participants to speak up. They may reveal account or product information that is not in sales force automation reports or campaign briefs.

The dealstorm meeting leader must also protect the "anxious

Andys," who worry about implementation issues or viability. In traditional brainstorming, we call them devil's advocates and consider them the enemy of creativity. But in dealstorming meetings, these folks are the guardians of the current process and, in many cases, prevent bad decisions from emerging.

Finally, the facilitator must protect ideas when they are first offered. Ed Catmull says that new ideas often arrive as an "ugly baby" and need time to develop into something beautiful through collaboration. Later, when the idea has been fleshed out and it's decision time, the suggestion will have to stand on its own.

Assertiveness: A strong facilitator is willing to handle the meeting hogs who try to dominate the conversation. Extroverts, by their nature, want to fill dead air with the sound of their own voices. Studies show that in the average six-person meeting, two people will do 70% of all the talking unless a strong facilitator tames them.[3]

The facilitator also needs to manage the disruptors, who either bring personality issues to the table or distract others with their devices or side conversations. Strong meeting leaders are willing to stand next to distractors or between those who engage in side conversations, an effective tactic for guiding participants back to the topic at hand. When a participant repeatedly acts dysfunctional in the meeting, the facilitator should be ready to confront him or her after the break and resolve the issue.

Facilitators also need to be persistent in order to prevent anyone from free riding on the work of others. According to Kellogg School of Management professor Leigh Thompson, "free riding is the number one complaint of work teams."[4] These people get all the credit for being on the team but are stone silent during meetings, especially when it's time to commit to working on next steps. Facilitators can conduct round-robin idea submissions, which require everyone to contribute, and otherwise make sure everyone is participating equally in a respectful and effective manner.

Another way to increase participation levels is to place an audio recorder in plain sight so that the meeting can be memorialized for later reference. In an experiment conducted by Professor Thompson, two groups were observed using this technique. The group that was being recorded had much higher levels of participation than the one that wasn't. In my experience, recording meetings also has a side benefit: nothing falls between the cracks in the event that the information master can't keep up with the pace of conversation.

When the sales team is less experienced or the stakes for wide meetings are especially high, sales leaders should consider offering trained in-house facilitators to assist problem owners during dealstorms. At Yahoo!, our chief sales officer designated my group, the ValueLab, to serve as researchers and facilitators for dealstorm meetings. It was a shared service that was on call for qualified opportunities. We helped the account executives write their deal briefs and made facilitation a center of excellence in our group. Over time, we became pretty proficient at leading cross-departmental meetings that produced measurable progress on big opportunities.

You'll find dedicated facilitator candidates in your training department or your sales enablement group. Trainers are unbiased about specific deals and are usually well trained in dealing with group dynamics. Sales enablement leads are close to account and service information and are often skilled at distilling multiple voices and ideas into action items. It's important for these facilitators to remember that the problem owner (account executive) remains the dealstorm's leader and that they are there as neutral support staff.

Designing the Meeting Space

The facilitator is responsible for sourcing and arranging the meeting space. While exotic locations or innovative room designs are often used for creative meetings, convenience improves attendance. Getting everyone to the meeting is priority number one. For ease of implementation, I like to use conference rooms (not open spaces in a common area) that are centrally located.

First things first: the meeting room must have an information- and idea-sharing space, visible to everyone in the room, where key points collected by the facilitator are recorded and displayed to the group by the information master. Flip charts or whiteboards are the best tools for this job. I've seen dealstorm meetings in which the information master compiled a list of nominated ideas on his or her laptop, projecting it on a screen. While that works, I like to go light on technology because it can distract from the meeting when there's a glitch.

There are three main lists that must be compiled during a dealstorm: ideas, issues, and action items. Facilitation expert Michael Wilkinson refers to these as parking boards.[5] This is where ideas or issues are headlined and then parked for the group's benefit. These boards help everyone know what's already been said, where it goes, and provides latecomers with a way to catch up on their own. Each board should have a title in capital letters across the top for easy identification.

If the facilitator plans on having participants do independent work at some point of the session, bring index cards or Post-it notes for them to jot ideas on and post on a wall or board.

Most conference rooms are not set up for collaborative meetings. The facilitator should arrive early enough to rearrange as necessary. The goal should be to eliminate barriers between people so they can engage and collaborate. According to Interactive Associates founder Dave Strauss, "The physical enrichment of a meeting room, especially the placement of chairs, has a powerful impact on a meeting. A semicircular seating arrangement opens up the space, and like a lens, focuses the energy of a group in a common direction, towards the [sharing space]."

Finally, it's important to make provisions for remote attendees. As a general rule, strive for 100% in-person attendance. Having people dial in dramatically reduces the quality of their participation and leads to a lot of awkward interruptions. I prefer that remote attendees dial in via video conferencing, Google Hangouts, or GoToMeeting, if needed. When a remote attendee wants to say something, he or she should raise a hand on screen or text the facilitator, who should be the only one checking his or her phone during the meeting.

Under no circumstance should a dealstorm commence if the problem owner and the sponsor are not physically present for the meeting, even if a strong facilitator is on hand. Their roles cannot be fulfilled remotely. After seeing a lot of meetings fall apart due to key attendees phoning in, I've come to the conclusion that it's better to reschedule the meeting than not have them in the room.

Key Responsibilities

As facilitator, you must ensure the meeting runs on time. The first dealstorm meeting should run between one and two hours, depending on the number of participants and complexity of the sales challenge. From the start time on the agenda to the promised adjournment, pay constant attention to the clock. If the meeting goes too long, it's an inconvenience to all participants and will hurt attendance at future meetings. Also, when meetings are running long, the end of the meeting gets rushed. That's usually where plans are made and action items are distributed, and you need time for that to go smoothly.

The facilitator is responsible for keeping everyone on point. If the discussion is centered on the problem space, deflect nonproblem points to the issues parking board or ask the participants to defer the point until later in the meeting, when you've turned to that topic. This is where assertiveness comes in handy. Altera's senior vice president of sales, Mark Nelson, who has sponsored many a dealstorm, has a saying about this: "Lead or be led."

Stay strong and keep everyone on task with the reminder that everyone is here to solve *this* sales challenge. Sometimes, participants will use the meeting as a platform to air non–deal-related grievances or bring up unrelated issues that have no place in the meeting. I've seen situations where long-standing arguments between silo dwellers erupted. Without strong facilitation, they descend into a meeting from hell for everyone involved. In this case, you must consistently remind participants about the purpose of the meeting, the value of everyone's time, and the importance of solving this challenge.

Finally, keep the meeting energetic and upbeat. Your meeting is only as high energy as you are. "When a facilitator leads a session with energy, the energy transfers to the topic," writes Michael Wilkinson in *The Secrets of Facilitation*, a book that greatly informed my consulting practice after Yahoo!.

Before I conducted dealstorm meetings for consulting clients, I always psyched myself up by playing high-energy music on my iPod. (This is a nod to Dwight Schrute from *The Office* sitcom, who always jammed on Metallica in the parking lot before big sales calls.) You see pro athletes do this during warm-ups, and as well as it works for them, it gets me going too. I loved to blast tunes from Bob Marley, Fatboy Slim, and Queen before my dealstorm sessions. Nothing gets me more pumped to pummel the competition than hearing "We are the champions. No time for losers!"

One surefire way to keep the tone of your meeting light is to infuse it with humor. Dr. David Roach and his colleagues at Arkansas Tech University conducted research to measure the impact of humor on a brainstorming meeting's effectiveness. While it had moderate impact on vague goals (easy tasks), "humor radically improved performance with stretch goals."[6] After all, when it comes to tension—which dealstorms may engender—laughter is the best medicine.

At Yahoo!, I loved to play the seminal scene from *Glengarry Glen Ross* ("Coffee's for closers! . . . Third place, you're fired!") to get everyone yukking it up prior to diving into the solutions discussion. Several of our executives humorously manipulated profile pictures of meeting attendees to kick off their meetings with a laugh. The key is to be creative but not mean spirited.

Now that we clearly understand the role of the problem owner and facilitator in the meeting, let's examine the key duties of the sponsor and information master. As you read the next section, put yourself in their shoes, even if you won't be serving in their capacity during the dealstorm. This section is useful to share with your sponsor and information master, who will fill those roles during your dealstorm.

As sponsor, you are responsible for supporting the facilitator by reinforcing the charter of the meeting. While the facilitator can handle disruptive meeting participants, high-ranking managers and executives are best handled by the sponsor, who will counsel them as a peer. As a leader, you should also remember to be one of the last to speak during interactive parts of the meeting. This ensures that no one is intimidated or deterred from sharing what he knows.

You also participate as a manager, commenting on implementation issues when it's time to consider finalists for the next best play and analyzing the facilitator's performance for feedback later. If the problem owner isn't facilitating the meeting, make sure he is driving the group's ability to reach consensus and commit to action items. After all, this is his account, and he needs to maintain a leadership role in the process.

As information master, you are responsible for capturing the essential thoughts from the meeting. Avoid editing any participant's submissions; instead, write exactly what was said. The writing must be very legible, and parking boards must have the title across the top of the flip chart or whiteboard.

In many of my dealstorm meetings, an artistically inclined information master brought ideas to life by drawing diagrams or illustrations to represent complex ideas or processes. It's a great way to reduce abstractions and produce more clarity for the entire group. Even simple time lines or process flow charts can bring ideas to life.

At the end of the meeting, collect all flip charts and take photos of the whiteboards so no information is lost. If the meeting is recorded, the information master should consider sending it off to an online transcription service. (For options, visit TimSanders.com/DealStorming.) All of the information should be immediately given to the problem owner.

Facilitating the Meeting

In facilitating a dealstorm meeting, you need to stick with the agenda, ask questions as opposed to making declarative statements, and keep your eyes and ears open at all times. If you stay with the process, and convince others to follow it, you'll almost always reach the primary goal of improving insights and options.

There are three basic types of dealstorming meetings: convenes, regroups, and reconvenes. The convene meeting is a kickoff meeting and will be the focus of this chapter. The recommended length is one to two hours, depending on the size of the group or opportunity and the complexity of the problem being tackled.

While agendas may vary with the situation, here's a standard layout:

1. Gathering time
2. Opening remarks
3. Introductions
4. Ground rules

5. Problem discussion
6. Solution discussion (open, narrow, close)
7. Action items
8. Review parking boards
9. Close

Don't bother sending out an agenda prior to the meeting; you want everyone to spend his or her time reading the deal brief and working on assignments. But you should post the agenda on a flip chart or a whiteboard in the meeting and, if possible, list start times for each section. I prefer this to handing out a printed agenda, which is usually doodled on or discarded later.

Gathering Time

Here's a technique for making the meeting magic from the start, from Michael Wilkinson, author of *The Secrets of Facilitation:* invite everyone to gather in the conference room or just outside of it ten minutes prior to the meeting start time.[7] Make sure this appears on the meeting confirmation email you send, along with the deal brief (e.g., "We'll gather outside Conference Room A12 at 9:50, and the meeting will convene at 10:00").

Prior to learning about this clever agenda hack, the majority of my dealstorm meetings ended up starting ten or so minutes late. Such is the nature of many company cultures. By including a gathering time, you send a strong signal to participants that the start time is firm and that they should be on time! If key participants don't show at gathering time, the problem owner has a chance to call or text them to make sure they are on the way.

The gathering time also allows casual, "how ya doin?" banter, which can create a comfort level between participants. If possible, have a snack and/or drinks available then so they can load up prior to the start time.

A few minutes prior to the start time, the facilitator should declare the two-minute warning or, as I like to do these days, shake the cowbell app on my smartphone. Don't let gathering time bleed over into your allotted meeting time.

Opening

Magic meetings have strong starts. To open the meeting, the problem owner should state the goal of the dealstorm project, as per the deal brief, and remind everyone why winning the deal is important. Be sure to explain the significance of the opportunity in the widest possible sense and, if appropriate, position it as a challenge for "all of us to find the truth, and rise to the occasion. Just like we always do."

Collaboration research suggests that nothing motivates people to reveal what they know and fully participate in discussions like a challenge to learn and solve as a matter of pride and personal excellence.[8] Competitive juices run a close second, so if that's your lever, use it! Remind the team who will win the deal if your company doesn't, how you feel about it, and what that means to everyone in the long run.

Next, explain that the primary purpose of this meeting is to gain information, insights, and potential ideas. Let them know that time is of the essence in any sales opportunity and that, in some cases, if the winning play won't emerge in the allotted time, you'll have to make the call on the next play, just like a team's head coach. This is important because this way no member of your dealstorm team will mistakenly think that the solutions are determined by committee and that any next step is up for a vote. In my experience, most nonsales dealstorm participants are happy to contribute to the project and not have to own the decision.

Finally, thank the participants for their valuable time spent on the project and, in particular, attending this meeting. Let them know that you and your sponsor have thought a lot about who was invited and that they were selected because they contribute equity to the group or that they deserve a place in the beginning of the process.

Introductions

The problem owner should also make the introductions, as she is the recruiter of the team and has the best visibility into each participant's potential contributions. These introductions set a context for the discussions that will happen later. When people hear comments from people they don't know, it's hard to accept them as legitimate unless they are aware of their relevant experience. Don't take more than a minute or so per attendee, as it's easy to get bogged down here and chew into problem- or solution-finding time. Start with why she is on the team and then explain what resource she has to offer.

At this point, it's a good idea to conduct an icebreaker exercise. At Yahoo!, I loved to ask meeting participants to tell us what their number one gift was that they used at work to solve problems. Sometimes, this led to helpful confessions, such as, "I'm not afraid to admit I don't know what I don't know," or "I can draw any thought on a whiteboard," or "I'm great at using search engines to prove or disprove anything I hear in a meeting," or my favorite, "I've got a great bullcrap detector!"

Another good icebreaker comes from my friend Ken Rutkowski, who conducts high-energy meetings with Los Angeles–area entrepreneurs and entertainment industry professionals. He calls it "speed to cool," in which attendees have thirty seconds to tell us something about themselves that makes them different from everyone else. These icebreakers force the participants to usher their first words to the group, hot on the heels of a generous introduction.

Ground Rules

At this point, the facilitator takes over the meeting (in the event the facilitator is not the problem owner). She will reveal the ground rules for the meeting, which should also be displayed on a flip chart.

A meeting without rules can easily descend into anarchy. While some might worry that rules inhibit creative thinking, the reality is that they actually help. According to facilitation expert Michael Wilkinson, the presence of effective ground rules not only improves the quality of ideas that come out of a meeting, they make the experience much less painful for everyone involved.

Over the last fifteen years, I've utilized various ground rules, looking for the ones that apply best to a deal-solving situation, where participants come from all departments and represent all levels of seniority. The following four work best for most situations:

1. *Ideas can come from anywhere.* This declaration is a part of the sales culture at many of the highest performing companies I've worked with. This rule means that no idea should be rejected due to its source. There are no experts who wholly own their domain. In fact, people far removed from it can have the most helpful perspective.

2. *Act on facts; research hunches.* It's very easy for the discussion to move toward gut instincts, rules of thumb, and anecdotal experiences. Without this rule, the debate often ends up with "trust me" as the trump card, often followed by discussions of one's expertise or whether his last hunch really played out. When someone believes that an assumption behind an idea

is logical, that doesn't mean it should necessarily drive a next best play. In some situations, I've created a research parking board where hunches are slated for background checks to verify their accuracy. In the case of out-of-the-box ideas, this rule recognizes that presumption lies with the status quo.

3. *Stay focused on the section at hand.* When you bring together creative/smart/energetic people, ideas come to them fast. Sometimes, it's easy for someone to jump straight to the solution or jump backward to the problem area toward the end of the discussion. The facilitator should emphasize that he will use the parking boards for any comments or ideas that don't belong in the current section of the meeting. This means that each section should be clearly announced by the facilitator, to open the floor to ideas that participants have been holding back out of respect for this rule.

4. *No distractions.* The facilitator should make it clear that the meeting won't welcome any interruptions, including ringing mobile phones, side conversations, laptop or tablet use by anyone other than the information master, or other such gadgety annoyances. If there are remote attendees, ask them to mute their lines unless they are going to make a comment or ask a question. It's important that this rule be laid out, giving participants the benefit of any doubt, as I don't like the ground rules part of the agenda to come across like the facilitator is the principal and the participants are unruly students.

Problem Discussion

At this point, the facilitator should refer to the problem question stated on the deal brief and invite a discussion about its accuracy in describing why the sales challenge exists. The meeting should allow for a minimum of fifteen minutes of discussion to make sure the real sticking point and its root cause are clear. In many cases, problem owners are too close to the situation to see what's really going on, and that's where the group dynamic can add a lot of value.

A few years ago, I saw firsthand how important a thorough vetting of "the problem" could be. A digital media sales team was pursuing a big advertising program with one of the Big Three Detroit-based automakers. They were stuck in the convince level, specifically on price, so the account executive assembled a diverse dealstorm team to help him break through.

During the previous meeting, the prospect responded to their pitch by telling them, "You'll need to beat our current ad partner's price to win our business!" The account executive stressed that their program was a rich media solution as opposed to the display advertising solution the current partner provided. Rich media inventory was not as vast as flat display, he explained, so it was impossible to match or beat the competition's price.

He and his manager deduced that the ad buyer's firmness on price and his objection to their pitch was likely due to a limited budget. In the deal brief, his problem question was "How might we convince [the car company] to find an additional $200,000 in their budget?"

When the problem discussion started, a marketing manager invited to the meeting challenged the problem owner's assumption. In her previous career, she worked at an ad agency that handled campaigns for car companies. "It's not a budget issue; it's a value issue," she explained. "Our proposal is a small part of their billion-dollar ad spend, so the extra 200k is a rounding error." This set off a vigorous debate about why "match their price" was the objection.

In the end, the account coordinator offered up a vital piece of insight: "They don't believe there's any performance difference between our rich media and their current provider's display ads." The account exec reminded her that they had showed two slides documenting their internal reporting of superior results with rich media . . . by 25%!

At this point, the marketing manager identified the true root problem: credibility. "No major advertiser will change providers because of your internal reporting! There's no way they can verify it." She explained that seasoned ad buyers have many tales of being burned by case studies and that usually you had to get into the account and prove yourself over time.

Once they could all agree that credibly differentiating their product was the real problem, they moved to the solution discussion, which quickly centered on working with a third party like Nielsen to verify their claims. Within three months, they repitched their program using third-party research to respond to the credibility concern. The ad buyer signed on at their price.

Problem finding is the foundation for developing winning solutions to sales challenges. As John Dewey once wrote, "A problem well stated is half solved."

Begin this section of the meeting by revealing the levels of the sale from Chapter 2 and then identifying exactly where the sale or renewal is stuck. (You can download a PowerPoint-friendly image at TimSanders.com/DealStorming.) It's helpful to educate the group, especially the nonsales participants, about the sales process so they understand that it's a complex game requiring multiple solutions along the way.

Usually, the sticking point is evident: if you can't make contact with the right influencer or decision maker, that's what should be addressed. If you can't conceive the right deal elements (products, services, offer), that's also pretty straightforward. However, the cause of the sticking point, the true problem, is another matter entirely. So far, you have identified a symptom and not its cause. And innovators, like the members of your dealstorming team, don't try to solve the symptom—they seek to cure its cause.

The facilitator should read the problem question from the deal brief and then invite a discussion about the cause behind it. The deal brief includes information on the attempts made to solve the problem by the problem owner, so a quick review sets the table for a closer look for the root cause of the sticking point.

One of the best questions the facilitator can ask at this point is, "Is there anything missing here?" This allows any participant to offer up information or even theories that can confirm or redirect the discussion. For existing account relationships, the facilitator should look to participants closest to the customer for feedback. If someone chirps in with something, the information master should record this feedback on the flip chart, creating a "Problem Ideas" sheet to track the discussion.

While this approach can sometimes bring the root cause(s) to the surface, the facilitator usually needs to employ a template (a repeatable exercise) to tease them out. As I mentioned in the last chapter, repeatedly asking "And why is that?" when faced with a sticking point can lead to discovering the problem behind the symptom.

In many sales challenges, there are several root causes behind the sticking point. In this case, it's important to identify them all and then prioritize which ones need to be solved to move forward. Another quality improvement template, the fishbone diagram exercise, works wonderfully in this case.

In the late 1960s, Kawasaki's Kaoru Ishikawa developed an exercise in which his managers identified and prioritized root causes of defects by creating a diagram that started with the surface problem, or sticking point, and worked backward to figure out possible causes, including several categories (think: buckets) and subcategories of cause. They grouped defect causes into people, process, machine, materials, measurement, and information categories, exploring where each one was breaking down. (These were the most appropriate categories for finding manufacturing quality problems.) Then they ranked their contribution to lower quality. In most situations, they isolated one or two specific causes that produced most of the problems.

Now let's apply this technique to a sales challenge. For a technology solutions provider, this might be a good fishbone:

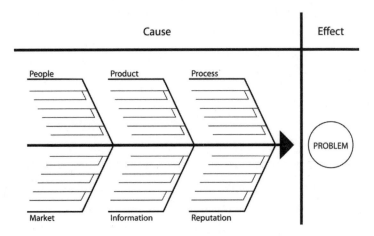

In most of my dealstorms, every cause connected to a sticking point or account crisis fits into one of these six categories.[9] Each one can apply to the buyer or the seller. As I mentioned previously, many of the problems that need to be solved in a stuck sale are internal. The people category refers to the individuals involved in buying as well as the individuals involved in selling to the prospect or working with the client. The product category includes all elements of the proposed deal, including services, billing, and reporting. Process concerns either how the buyer does business or how the seller pursues deals and contracts them. Market refers to economic conditions, competition (either the buyer's or the seller's) and proposed, recent, or likely mergers or acquisitions that can affect the selling process. Information includes what the buyer knows, needs to know, or has supplied the seller. It also includes internal information the sellers have that influences their tactics, proposed deal, or deal structure. Reputation involves the seller's track record in terms of product or service quality as well as corporate social responsibility. It can also include the buyer's track record in terms of how they pay their bills or treat vendors, which comes into play in the contract phase.

In some situations, you may find that there are other categories that influence your deals getting stuck or accounts going south. (Download the above or a blank category fishbone at TimSanders.com/ Dealstorming.)

In many dealstorms, the fishbone diagram exercise sparks discussions that reveal root causes behind the dominant difficulty. That's why the diagram includes a drop-down line underneath each category cause. Also, you'll often find that there are multiple causes behind your problem. This can mean that there might be more than one problem that will need to be solved to get past a single sticking point— and that's OK. If you don't attempt this exercise, you could eliminate one cause but still not have a solution that takes you to the next level of the sale.

Another problem-finding exercise is to discuss personality attributes of people in the influence map section of the deal brief. Whether it's the current contact, key influencers, or decision makers, their attitudes, beliefs, and backgrounds can all be root causes of the sticking point. If one of your resources has a similar job or history to a problem prospect, his or her insights may be quite revealing. If you've assigned someone a research dig into one of these people, have her briefly summarize relevant findings.

Finally, the root cause can sometimes be found by locating an analogous situation in which the same symptom appeared as a sticking point. It could be a previous sales situation, either within the same industry or involving similar personalities. In this case, a tenured sponsor, fellow account exec, or coordinator might have revealing insights that transfer to the current situation.

It's important for the facilitator to drive consensus on the root cause of the problem before moving to the solution discussion. And please make note if you're rushing through this problem discussion for the sake of getting through your agenda items. If the discussion takes more than fifteen minutes, it's more of a reflection of the problem's complexity than a misguided agenda. Take your time. As David Strauss points out in *Making Collaboration Work*, "If you can't agree on the problem, you won't agree on the solution."

The Solution Discussion

This is the heart of the dealstorm meeting, where next best plays are nominated, debated, and agreed on. At this point, the facilitator announces that the problem-solving portion of the meeting is starting and does a quick check to identify how much time is left. Explain that the goal is to find the next best play as well as a backup option if after-meeting verification doesn't support the first play as a viable move. Looking for more than one idea overcomes the group dynamic known as the primacy effect, "the strong tendency to be attracted to the first option that is suggested," which can often lead to an incomplete exploration for the right solution.[10]

In this stage of the meeting, the facilitator should explain the solution discussion process, which consists of three distinct parts: opening, narrowing and closing. The first part of the discussion is the opening, in which ideas are nominated with some explanation but no debate. Next comes narrowing, in which ideas are vetted for solvency, doability, and costs. Finally comes closing, in which options are rated or ranked and then a decision is made on the winner and the backup.

During the solution discussion, enforce this process firmly, reminding everyone of process as necessary. Anything not related to a solution should be parked on the issues parking board. The information master should headline options on the idea parking board, leaving room underneath each entry for more notes or votes later.

A good first step is to ask the group, "Is there anything inside the box we can do? Is there a best practice that we can apply here?" I learned this trick at Yahoo!, where vigorous root cause discussions often revealed that we had a solution in hand we'd never tried because we were trying to solve the wrong problem. When insider ideas are nominated, the facilitator should ask the problem owner, "Have we tried that in full? What happened? Anything changed since then?" This isn't an invitation to debate the idea but, instead, confirm that the existing approach isn't going to take the team to the next level.

Next comes the out-of-the-box discussion in which the group nominates novel approaches.

Prior to calling for ideas, review the constraints section in the deal brief. Identifying constraints up front helps resources avoid suggesting any ideas that are not an option. Such constraints may include budget, time, resources, discounting or bonus limits, or boundaries. It's important for the facilitator to get agreement from the group that these are real constraints and not just the costs of innovation. Next, review the resources section so everyone in the room is aware of what they can leverage in solving the problem.

At this point, ask for or collect submissions and list them on the ideas board. In the event there are dominant extroverts in the room or potentially helpful introverts attending, consider an alternative to going around the room for verbal suggestions. Options include brain writing—writing ideas on index cards or Post-it notes—or cyberstorming—submitting ideas electronically on a shareable document or cloud-based service for the information master to organize and list. (Visit TimSanders.com/DealStorming for a list of resources.)

In the prepare stage, if applicable, problem owners encourage some or all of the resources to bring ideas to the meeting based on their review of the deal brief. As mentioned in the last chapter, the problem owner should also have a few suggestions in his back pocket to offer up in case the call for ideas fails to produce any from the group. Getting the first idea on the table is the key to inspiring other team members to make creative connections or share ideas they were too timid to offer up for discussion.

In the event the problem owner, acting as facilitator, nominates an idea, according to Leadership Strategies' Michael Wilkinson, she should "float" the idea, asking the group, "What would be the benefits to doing this?" It's important that the team knows you didn't come into the meeting set on any one idea. It's also important that facilitators stay as neutral as possible on ideas.

There are templates and exercises you can use to bring out ideas in the event the listing process didn't reveal several good options. The first one is the analog exercise, used at companies such as RCA, Singer, and Kimberly-Clark. This exercise is known in innovation circles as synectics, loosely meaning "to work together from the outside."[11] In this exercise, the facilitator asks the team to name a similar situation to this root cause or problem situation. Let's take the example of an account stuck in the conceive phase as a result of the account executive not having enough information about the customer's operations (the root cause). In this scenario, the group should find an analog—another situation where getting to the info in the vault was required. In one of my dealstorms, a resource suggested that a physician trying to diagnose a patient without having direct access to the patient or his medical records was analogous to a root cause that had been identified. In another meeting, a resource brought up police trying to solve a crime where uncooperative witnesses were involved. In both situations, the facilitator then asked, "Well, how should they proceed?" As the group deliberated, ideas surfaced about the fictional situations that were mutually relevant to the sales challenge at hand.

Imagineering is another template I use with success. In *Applied Imagination,* Alex Osborn introduced the concept as "letting your imagination soar, then engineering it down to earth."[12] This involves looking at an imaginary situation, then analyzing how the problem would be solved in that context. For example, the group could imagine that the sales challenge was solved, then work backward to figure out what made the difference. If you are trying to get past the convince level, you could start with the prospect asking for the contract, then analyzing what it took to get him or her over the hump. This mental exercise can reveal obvious solutions that, until that moment, had never been spotted.

Another Imagineering approach involves thinking about imaginary scenarios, such as what would our best competitor do in this situation to solve the problem? This is when the group's diversity might really add value. I've witnessed situations in which really strong ideas emerged when a resource was freed from the false constraints of his own company, taking on the mindset, agility, or courage of a top competitor.

Scenario planning is an exercise in which two or more futures are imagined and then solutions are sought that work in either situation. Pierre Wack pioneered this exercise as "a way of liberating people's insights" while leading innovation teams at Royal Dutch Shell.[13] At Toyota, for example, while exploring what to do if the price of oil skyrocketed (one scenario) or if the world's consumers became very ecologically oriented (a second scenario), the core idea of the hybrid Prius was conceived.

At Yahoo!, I adapted the scenario-planning template when problem solving a strategic marketing partnership with Hewlett-Packard. I'd assembled a large dealstorm team, including several high-ranking HP participants. After two days of presenting our services to HP, we were at an impasse. We couldn't convince them we had marketing solutions that could provide significant value.

I offered to fetch lunch for the group while they ran through an exercise. I asked them to pretend that Carly Fiorina (HP's CEO at the time) had just announced that they were buying Yahoo! for thirty billion dollars and that this group's assignment was to make the merger accretive. "If you bought Yahoo!," I asked my HP dealstormers, "what would you do with our resources and capabilities to recoup the cash?" When I returned forty-five minutes later, the HP team had come up with over a dozen ideas, which turned out to be the basis of a multimillion-dollar deal.

Another template that can drive ideation is known as the SIT method, which stands for Systemic Inventive Thinking. Its premise is that most problems are solved through the exercise of subtraction, addition, multiplication, or division.

For subtraction, "the trick is to eliminate something previously thought of as necessary."[14] In one dealstorm where I was advising a defense contractor as they prepared their final pitch to a government IT buyer, we subtracted the PowerPoint presentation from the pitch process and instead invested forty-five minutes in a question-and-answer session, leaving behind a printed copy of the slides that the prospect could then peruse. Several sales leads in the room freaked out, exclaiming, "We've never pitched without one!" But in fact, the approach dramatically increased the engagement of the prospect, getting them to reveal key buying triggers and moving the conversation to contract.

Addition is the act of adding components to the approach. I've been in situations where my team was stuck trying to make the right contact, so adding more targets ended up solving the problem. In the case of the Allegis contract problem, Alyssa added a new provision for a technical lead, which solved the prepayment impasse.

Multiplication involves creating several copies or instances of an element of your deal (e.g., prospecting tactic, research task, product, service, presentation item, contractual term). This approach has worked with teams trying to conceive the deal, where several rounds of due diligence were conducted, revealing key information for applying the right mix of products. In one situation where I was working with a software company that was stuck trying to convince the prospect to invest three million dollars into an annual license, we increased the term to five years, which allowed us to create better price points and add a lot more services, given the length of commitment.

Division is the act of breaking down a component into its parts. When working through the contact phase, I've seen teams divide and conquer by approaching technology, finance, and business operations separately. Once, when I was consulting with a payroll services company that was trying to save a multimillion-dollar omnibus deal, we reduced our downside by breaking it up into more than a dozen deals, based on the customer's geographical regions. In the end, billings actually increased.

After identifying the right exercise for the situation, one option is to break the team into small groups and have them choose a group leader and a scribe to record their collective ideas. Groups should be given a relatively short period of time to discuss their ideas and then have the leader present their findings to the whole dealstorm team.

In the case of Imagineering or Systemic Inventive Thinking, if the team is large enough, the facilitator can use small groups as a way of generating well-thought-out ideas quickly and giving everyone a chance to participate. For example, different groups could ideate based on different scenarios. In the case of SIT, four groups could use subtract, add, multiply, or divide as the parameters for their ideations.

It's very important that you, as facilitator, ensure that the opening part of the solution discussion be completed with at least twenty minutes left in the meeting. Announce time checks, and in the event of small group breakouts, plan accordingly.

When the ideas are collected, announce that the narrowing

portion of the discussion has begun. Refer to the ideas board, and review each headline, asking the resource who offered it up, "Why does this work?" and "What's your key assumption behind it?" Then open the floor to the group for any questions or objections to the idea's solvency, doability, or costs.

Be vigilant in ensuring that naysayers are "hard on ideas, but soft on people," as Wilkinson recommends, and that generalities such as "It'll never work" or "That's a dumb idea" are converted into very specific points.[15]

In many cases, when ideas show promise but also contain flaws, you should encourage participants to build on ideas. In Pixar culture, this is called plussing. This tactic requires someone with an objection to an idea to suggest how to make it better. For example, one of my technology solutions clients created a dealstorm to pursue a Fortune 100 prospect. They were stuck in the conceive level because they couldn't get the prospect to reveal enough information about their technology stack (hardware, software, third-party vendors) to craft recommendations and calculate the value proposition in terms of savings. One of the team members from research suggested that they hold a "share and learn" seminar at headquarters, where high-ranking executives from both companies would sit on a panel to discuss future trends in technology and how they are leveraging them. In his mind, this could lead to valuable insights to help conceive the deal.

A marketing manager in the meeting worried that this wouldn't be enough to entice the prospect's executives or technology managers to take the time to attend. Following the plussing rule, he said, "Yes, and we should hire a well-known business author to be the moderator for the panel!" The team responded positively to this suggestion, realizing it could add sizzle to the event.

A finance director in the meeting feared that this could dramatically add to the cost of the sale without any guarantee that it would excite the prospects enough to attend and be forthcoming about how they ran their business. To protect the company's investment, he suggested that they first survey prospect contacts to find out what books they were reading, sharing, and talking about. By investing in a moderator that they knew the prospect respected, the panel discussion would be well attended and lead to high levels of engagement. This turned out to be the winning play. The sales leader then organized a breakthrough event where the prospect revealed the nitty-gritty on what they used, who they worked with, and what they were researching for future application.

To quickly identify finalists for the next portion of the discussion, ask the group to help classify the idea as hot, potential, or problematic by show of hands. The information master should create a new flip chart, labeled "Finals," to contain the short list of potential solutions.

During the closing portion of the meeting (a span of ten minutes), invite the group to rate the top ideas. The facilitator can pass out adhesive dots and direct participants to place them on the sheets listing their favorite solution. Or you can ask each participant to go up to the finals flip chart and give each idea a score from 1 to 10, with 10 being the best score. If the meeting's time is running out or the nominated ideas need follow-up research to vet for effectiveness, the problem owner and sponsor can confer after the event and pick an idea from the finals flip chart themselves. In the event you plan to go that route, make sure you establish early on that you two will ultimately choose the next best play from the short list that the group creates.

If possible, it's desirable to generate buy-in from the participants on the next best play. But consensus isn't always possible—and in the case consensus isn't reached, the problem owner and sponsor will serve as fallback deciders.

Consensus isn't about everyone loving the idea but instead making sure that everyone can live with it later. This might involve some negotiations, in which the facilitator asks detractors of the next best play idea, "What would it take to live with this idea?" This forces them to build upon ideas rather than rejecting them outright.

The value of driving consensus is that it generates team kinship, satisfaction in the meeting's outcome, and a sense that everyone's input is valued. In the case of those who will be required to deliver on the deal after it's signed, it's key that they be on board with next steps, especially in solving the conceive level, where service levels will be set and promises will be made to the prospect.

It's important to point out that the first dealstorming meeting doesn't always end with the identification or adoption of a winning idea. Perhaps we were lacking information that we didn't know we needed, or we couldn't verify key assumptions or answer implementation issues with the group at hand. While the goal of the meeting is to hatch a plan of action, this won't always happen. But each and every time, if the prep work and facilitation are strong enough, the meeting does produce valuable insights. In that event, the problem owner should thank the group for their contributions, outline action items, and, if necessary, schedule another dealstorm session.

In the final minutes of the meeting, the facilitator conducts the actions items portion of the agenda. Whether the action items are research or acting on the decisions made during the meeting, the problem owner ultimately is responsible for the after-meeting work. However, he may canvass the room, asking for volunteers to assist with these tasks. In many cases, certain resources are in a good position to act on ideas or conduct necessary research to verify the next best play or the backup play.

The information master should create a new flip chart labeled "Action Items," outlining actions and who is responsible for them. Under no circumstance should someone outside of the meeting be assigned any work. This is a prescription for nonexecution—and a little resentment, too.

The facilitator should then review the issues parking board, where nonagenda items were recorded in the course of the meeting. Ask the room if there's any required follow-up on that board, and if so, who owns the work. Normally, this isn't the responsibility of the problem owner, who should be laser focused on moving the deal or account save to the next level.

Finally, the problem owner should conclude the meeting by thanking the group for their time and participation. He or she should remind everyone of the importance of solving the challenge. As I mentioned, in many cases, the dealstorm meeting creates more questions than answers—but that's a good thing. Here again, we call on the power of incubation as the problem owner asks everyone to consider the problem, its cause, and the potential solutions to it over the coming days and weeks. I've often concluded my dealstorms by telling the participants, "As you drive to work, eat lunch in the cafeteria, or watch TV, think about this challenge. Consider the problem space and the ideas we've thrown around today. If you come up with anything, please send an email to me." You'd be surprised how much great information and new ideas came later from the resources who couldn't stop thinking about the problem and eventually cracked the code for the problem owner. Even though the meeting itself is important, if conducted correctly it's just the starting point for truly innovative thinking by the whole team.

CHAPTER 7

Cleaning Up After the 'Storm

J ohn Livesay built up a reputation at *W* magazine as a person of action, or more specifically, a flurry of postmeeting activity. Over the course of his decade-plus career in advertising sales at the company, he has organized, facilitated, and executed dozens of deal-storm meetings.

"I'm obsessed with minding the details that keep the deal moving forward," he told me. He blocks out an hour after facilitating a meeting or conference call to gather up notes, then distills them all into an email that he immediately sends out to all participants. "It's about making sure we are all on the same page," he explained. "Quick and specific follow-up is essential so everyone knows what the action items are for each person and how that moves us along towards the common goal: winning."

He spends the first post-dealstorm days verifying claims, hunting down required information, and then making plans for action. Frequently, he'll phone dealstorm team members and ask them if they've had any additional thoughts or to confirm that they can or will deliver on their assignments. He gives everyone concrete time lines and then marches diligently to them "to bring the ideas from the meeting to life."

His goal is to build, vet, and launch the solution quickly and then step back to measure deal progress and then plan next steps. "My role is a hybrid of coach and producer," John says. "We need to make progress, but at the same time keep the team together and motivated. Because there will be more meetings or calls to come!"

John's signature tactic is weekly reporting to the deal team, focused on the progress that's being made. "People love structure. They want to know how the project is coming along. Closing the loop keeps the team together."

This underscores an important point: the ideas from a dealstorm are worthless unless they are acted upon, analyzed, and improved. The quality of postmeeting follow-up is seismically more influential to the outcome than the magic that happened in the room or the enthusiasm that oozed out of it afterward. "There is no good or bad sales organization," says Mark Schmitz, COO at SAP Cloud, "just which ones can execute the best."

The execution step in the dealstorming process involves more than just "doing what we agreed to do." After a good storm, there is rainfall (ideas), debris (loose ends) and blue skies (opportunity). While meetings can produce strong ideas, and many participants come well prepared, their outputs are still a work in progress.

There are three critical steps to the solid execution of a collaborative idea: (1) confirm what was decided and agreed upon; (2) verify the assumptions and claims made about key issues, such as cause and solution; and (3) implement the winning idea methodically and in such a way that allows for a test–iterate–launch approach, if possible.

Confirm

As problem owner, your first responsibility after a meeting is to confirm its key takeaways and action items with all of its participants. Try as you might, you can miss critical details or nuances that happened in a dealstorm meeting. Even if the end-of-meeting review is crystal clear about what happened in the 'storm and what's up next, people walk out of the room and back to their lives, and without follow-up on your part, nothing gets done. According to John Livesay, "This is the most important action step because it keeps everyone involved in the process and opens the door to a wider conversation."

Soon after the meeting, review the parking boards and gather up the key insights, decisions, issues, and action items that were agreed on. If the meeting was recorded, the file should be submitted to a transcription service to create a written account of the conversation. (See TimSanders.com/DealStorming.)

After reviewing all the information, send an email to every meeting participant, reviewing the decisions made and the action items agreed upon, including a time line for action. (If your information master is heavily involved, review this update with her first.) While sending group emails is efficient, and can give every participant each other's contact information, they can lead to "reply all" frenzies ("Thanks!" "Me too!" "That was fun!") that can annoy participants who already have a hundred emails in their inboxes. So, time permitting, send dealstorm participants individual emails in which the meeting summary is the same, but the postmeeting assignment review is personalized to the recipient. In some cases, there will be meeting attendees who aren't on the hook for anything, and that's OK because the time you take to send them individual emails shows how much you value their involvement.

The confirmation email should contain two additional elements: a revised deal brief and a request for continued consideration. In almost every case, meetings will produce new information for you or the information master to add to the deal brief. Perhaps you found a new root cause, which creates an entirely new problem statement. Or the review of the influence map revealed new players or insightful personality attributes. At the end of the deal brief, the meeting assignment should be replaced with outstanding action items, transparently listing who has agreed to do what (and when).

The updated deal brief can be a Word document (make sure to add the date to the file name to prevent confusion) or a cloud-based document that allows for everyone's continued edits or inputs. It's important to add this document to sales force automation, filed under the prospective or current account. This can be a valuable asset for associates in different parts of your company working with the same account.

The follow-up email should end with an open door to continued feedback and postmeeting thoughts. Ask each resource to consider the problem and its root cause over the coming days, especially when doing something non–work related. In many situations, if your resources continue to ponder the problem after your meetings, they will come up with ideas or observations much more useful than they did in real time.

I can't emphasize enough how crucial it is for you to complete the confirmation step in a relatively short period of time. This is particularly relevant for dealstorms that include millennials who expect quick feedback; however, regardless of generation, everyone expects to hear follow-up sooner than later. In *Creative Conspiracy,* Leigh Thompson puts it this way: "For a state of team flow and complete engagement to occur, the team needs immediate feedback."

Verify

The good news is that your dealstorm meeting has likely hatched a plan of action. The reality is that there are a series of assumptions that the action plan is based on that you need to verify right away. Most project mistakes occur because we trust too much and double-check too little. Think of assumptions as the foundation of any strategy. It only takes a few faulty beams to bring the house down under any sort of weight.

You might have noticed that I did not suggest fact-checking or any type of verification process during the meeting. That was by design; it would slow down the meeting, as various participants would feel inclined to query every statement made during the discussion. The in-room verification process would also inhibit others from offering any educated guesses or making any statements that they aren't 100% sure about.

Review your meeting outputs, starting with the problem discussion. Review your notes or the transcript from the meeting and identify key assumptions behind the root cause the group agreed on. If there were several potential causes, review the ranking or weighting that was given to them, again, isolating their assumptions. If one of the meeting attendees has access to the required information, email or call him to secure it. Otherwise, use your internal resources or online repositories to conduct this step of the process.

In some cases, you should meet with your sponsor to gather her opinion about the decisions made and what verification steps you should take next. As she is more senior in the organization, she'll often know "where the bones are buried" or have pretty good hunches about where you can find the proof points you need to take action.

As you verify the next best play (assuming you decided on one), separate your analysis of the solvency of the idea from its implementation issues. If it doesn't have an impact on the sticking point, you don't need to spend the time exploring whether it's doable.

Many assumptions are based on historical facts, either within the account, the industry, or your company's past efforts. In some cases, it's as easy as looking it up in sales force automation. In others, you'll have to make several phone calls or write a batch of emails to double-check what happened back when.

Sometimes the assumption behind an idea is that "it seems logical" or "I have a gut instinct that this will work." In this case, you need to consider the source. During several dealstorm meetings, a charismatic and emphatic resource can convince everyone in the room that a certain approach will work. Though the facilitator may evoke ground rule #2 (act on facts; research hunches), sometimes the seniority or expertise of the nominating participant is perceived as proof positive.

In the case of the nonhistorical and nonempirical assumptions, you will need to solicit opinions from your sponsor, fellow account executives you trust, and subject matter experts inside the company, as well as trusted members at the prospect company. In many cases, you'll get answers that yield leads to measurable assumptions you can chase down.

In the event that your research reveals that the next best play turns out to be based on faulty assumptions or is getting push back from management, you should begin vetting the backup play, if there is one. In many dealstorms I've run, the group anchored around the first idea (remember the primacy effect?), and that's why I suggested capturing an alternative solution, just in case. Take the same approach: look for historical proof, facts and figures, and if all else fails, talk to experts—those "in the know."

If your meeting ended with several potential solutions but no consensus on the winner, you'll need to do the assumption check on all ideas and then regroup the dealstorm team to discuss findings and drive toward consensus. In the event you don't have the time to organize another meeting, share the results with your sponsor to collaboratively decide on which, if any, are viable solutions to pursue. In any event, you should brief everyone on the team by email as to your thoughts on the next best play, and leave the door open for their feedback.

The next verification step is to identify and resolve any implementation issues that will preclude the plan from coming to life. They could be issues related to policy, either in the sales group or other parts of the company such as finance, legal, IT, or partner relations. To implement the idea, you may need to get approval or commitment for required resources, such as budget, labor, or executive support. During this step, your sponsor is your key partner. This is her most important role in the dealstorm process, and she's most qualified to help.

When the next play involves significant work outside of the sales group—such as development of financials, creative design, computer coding, etc.—your team members may need to hold meetings or have conversations with their department managers or potential working partners to verify that the resources are available. If possible, the problem owner should attend those meetings to answer questions about the value of the account or issues related to the sticking point. Often the need for such an internal meeting or conversation will come up at the end of the dealstorm meeting, during the action items conversation. The problem owner should make sure the team member understands the urgency of the situation and that it must not wait until their next staff meeting for discussion.

The final stage of idea consideration is to look for downsides. In many cases, these caveats were offered up in the narrowing part of the solution discussion. As with the ideas, the anticipated disadvantages to a plan are also based on assumptions that you can verify. Be particularly vigilant about those downsides that can degrade internal or external relationships, as they are hard to rebuild later. If the risks are merely financial or technical, use cost-benefit analysis to determine whether you should still take the leap or pursue a new direction.

In the event that assumptions break down, internal resources for the next play aren't available, the solutions don't look viable, or you've uncovered new information that could change the team's perspective about the situation, you should call a regroup meeting. This should be a shorter dealstorming meeting, held as soon as possible. The problem owner should update the deal brief to include findings from the verification process, new information strategic to the situation, or news events that affect the prospect company. The revised deal brief should be sent out via email at least one day prior to the regroup. The average regroup should not exceed forty-five minutes, shorter than a convene meeting, but still requires facilitation to be effective. While inviting everyone from the original meeting is good form, it's OK if it's slightly smaller, so long as the key individuals with subject matter expertise or a stake in the outcome are present. The agenda is simple: present findings, reopen the problem and solutions discussions, and discuss next best play options.

Sometimes, the best ideas come from this get together, as your team's incubation period liberated their individual creativity and willingness to offer up suggestions or debate ideas. Use fresh parking boards and take copious notes, and confirm key decisions and action steps immediately after the meeting. Pay close attention to key assumptions during the regroup, as much of your postmeeting research will immediately be helpful in the discussion.

After the meeting, repeat the entire verification cycle. When you've made it through the gauntlet of fact checking, idea bouncing, and research, you now have a plan of action. Still, you'll need to grit your teeth because, as management guru Peter Drucker said, "Plans are only good intentions unless they immediately degenerate into hard work."

In the event that you and your sponsor make a decision on the next best play outside of a dealstorm meeting, make sure to send out an email to all participants, letting them know why you've decided on this course of action. In the email, isolate the insights from the meeting that assisted you in finding the final solution, helping everyone on the team to realize the value of the process. Facilitation expert Michael Wilkinson suggests that you should first acknowledge the potential benefits from the idea the group agreed upon, and then proceed to demonstrate how the verification process suggested it wasn't the right plan. "This shows everyone respect for their involvement in the process," he explained. That's important, too, because in a complex sales challenge, you'll need this team to stay engaged to work on future sticking points. Reaching out after the initial convene meeting, or after a regroup, is a small gesture that goes far.

Implement

With plan in hand, it's now time to seek out or check the availability of all resources required to build the solution. In the event you're looking to test a solution in the conceive level, perhaps a financial analyst needs to run a return on investment formula or create a pricing matrix. For a convince-level solution, creative presentation elements might be required. Hopefully, team members are doing this work, but in my experience there are always additional resources required to complete the plan.

Once you're assured of the resources, craft a schedule of events detailing the deadline by which each action is slated to occur. A clear time line ensures quality work in execution as well as a sense of urgency. Review this with your sponsor to make sure that the approach remains viable and that the timing is right. He may also help you secure any outstanding resources at the last minute.

If possible, you or your resource should build a prototype of the solution. For a contact strategy, this could be a flow chart of a new route to gain access to key decision makers or influencers. For a conceive solution, the prototype could be a return on investment formula or down and dirty spreadsheet that itemizes the potential customer benefits from your service. For a convince-level idea, you might create a drawing of how your proposed service works or a crude PowerPoint mock-up of the end product, including customization. For a contract-level problem, it could be a draft of the new language posted on a flip chart.

The key in prototyping is to create a visual representation of a concept. *In Search of Excellence* author Tom Peters often said that the value of a prototype is that someone can reply, "That's not it," because prototypes eliminate the abstraction of ideas—often expressed verbally. During Yahoo! dealstorms, I would often hang a sign on the wall featuring an IDEO design mantra that echoed this sentiment: "A prototype is worth a thousand meetings."

Share the prototype with relevant team members immediately either via email or at a regroup meeting, to make sure it's tracking with the envisioned solution. Sharing it with dealstorm participants usually generates immediate insights, saving you or your resource a lot of time in the final build of the finished work. An energy services company ran a dealstorm while stuck in the conceive stage with a prospect, and found themselves in a long discussion about various "next step" options. An engineer drew a flow chart on the whiteboard, prototyping how resources would be distributed to the client and what would trigger additional costs. By being able to see the proposed service and suggest modifications to it specifically, the group was able to come to consensus on the next play in less than thirty minutes—a speed record for their culture.

Organize feedback on the prototypes via email or quick phone calls, make necessary adjustments, and then share them again, widely.

When the solution is built, polished and ready to launch, there's a final step that reduces the risk and in many cases, leads to the winning tweak: the test.

As I mentioned earlier, I started out my professional career managing quality circles, a problem-solving technique for manufacturers facing quality control issues. We followed the Deming Cycle[1] of continual improvement, which meant that when we were cleared for implementation, we always attempted to test the final solution prior to fully launching it plantwide. This was known as the "test and scale" approach, which is widely used today in advertising, technology, and process improvement.

One way to do this is to employ what I call the whisper test. This requires a little nuance because in many situations the reveal of the solution is done in a meeting or by "throwing it over the wall" to the prospect or client. The trick is to "whisper," or informally present, the idea to a trusted contact at your prospect company, someone who is willing to be a sounding board for ideas in progress. When you present the idea, let her know that it's not final, not to be shared yet, and that you greatly appreciate her help in "getting this into the right shape" for a formal presentation later. This will allow you to gain valuable feedback prior to committing to an idea with collateral that locks it in.

When I was consulting with a technology outsourcing company, the dealstorm team had concocted an innovative approach to managing a prospect's real estate that would rely on satellite-based cameras to monitor external maintenance requirements and parking lot capacity. Given the team had some reservations about the cutting-edge technology at the heart of the plan, the account executive approached her trusted contact at the prospect face to face and shared prototypes of the map grids, a pricing formula for the service, and creative elements for the formal presentation, explaining that it was a work in progress. He then asked the trusted contact, "If we present this to your CFO, CTO, and finance VP, will that dog hunt?" It turns out that the prospect's chief technology officer was a fan of Google Earth, which relied on the same technology, but the chief financial officer was more old school and preferred on-the-ground surveillance of his assets. Presenting a remote monitoring plan to him would likely freak him out and cause him to worry that the whole project was too high-tech for his taste.

The resulting feedback led to a tweak in the plan. The final proposal included a combination of periodic physical inspection and routine satellite based monitoring that would satisfy both parties. Presented with this prototyped and tested plan, the CFO and the CTO came on board immediately.

What if you have no prospect or client side contact to shop a potential solution to? At managed cloud services company Firehost, sales leader Jim Hilbert finds a mirror of the decision maker to whom he can "virtually pitch." Because his team sells to chief information security officers, he solicits his CISO for the trial run of the prototype of the finished product. While the scenario planning exercise is conducted in-house, the mirror's response often reflects what the prospect might think or say about it.

A final way to test an idea is to locate an opportunity in the sales pipeline with a lookalike sticking point and then try the solution to see whether it moves the deal forward. This is a tactic that one of my television network clients often took when attempting out-of-the-norm packaging of ad units. For example, in one deal situation, the team located a previous example of that ad package in its sales automation system, talked to the account executive about how the prospect reacted to it, and what finally happened. They found out that the prospect needed to see the ad effectiveness results first, before being presented the creative on the actual ads along with their nifty features. This helped the prospect overcome the complexity of ad choices and focus attention on which package would sell the most. It doesn't mean ideas that work with previous prospects always scale to the situation, but often the insights gained from real-world testing led to last-minute improvements.

With the final solution in hand, the problem owner implements the play with the prospect or client. The play to break through the contact level is often conducted by the sales rep, unless the prescription requires additional players (such as an executive or a coworker with a similar title as the target prospect). For conceive-level plays, much of the work occurs behind the scenes, as a working group led by the problem owner determines, shapes, and adds into a proposal the elements of the deal and why each element produces value. For convince, the implementation involves conducting research to create proof points or developing creative elements for the next presentation or deliverable. For contract, implementation involves a redraft of the agreement and/or conference calls or meetings to discuss changes to terms or the reasons they should stay the same.

In many cases, the approach that the dealstorm leads to is novel, something the company's never tried before in the market. But that's not something you should ever lead with during a meeting or presentation! "Well, this is certainly a new thing for us . . . but here it goes," will always alert the Spidey sense in the prospect and cause him to look for holes or be on guard for trickery.

I always tell problem owners, "You've done great work; now present it with pride as if it's something you do every day." When implementing an especially novel or unexpected play, tell your prospects that you've built a collaborative team around this potential relationship and that their work led to these creative yet thoughtful results. This disclosure helps even the most conservative prospects buy in to innovative approaches on your part. They usually respect the effort you and your team have put into your work.

Analyze

Frank Lloyd Wright once wrote, "Get the habit of analysis—analysis will in time enable synthesis to become your habit of mind." His point was that if we take time to analyze our actions and their results, we'll learn how to fold the old and the new into remarkable solutions.

Great dealstormers analyze the effectiveness of their efforts thoroughly. The act of looking objectively at your work's output will boost your ability to improve at every stage of the process.

If the solution involves a live presentation to the prospect, make an immediate read on the prospect's reaction to it, noting verbal feedback, body language, and facial expressions. While the initial reaction to an idea may not be determinative to the ultimate result, you can still learn a lot from paying close attention. Your prospect may exclaim, "That's the ticket!" or more subtly express satisfaction, such as nodding or carefully taking notes. You can also read their faces with a high degree of accuracy to gauge the emotions of surprise, delight, or even contempt. (See TimSanders.com/7faces.)

Many of the potential downsides your team might have identified in the meeting have to do with feelings and not fiscal realities, so measuring emotional reactions to your approach is important. In many cases, creative solutions are, by their nature, unsettling or disruptive, but the good ones produce "aha" moments in others that you can read like a book.

When looking at the effectiveness of your efforts, start by revisiting the root cause the dealstorm team agreed on during the meeting. Was this root cause eliminated by your solution? Or when it went away, did another problem pop up?

At Cox Media Group, the sales culture emphasizes the concept of contracting, of gaining little agreements or commitments to the next level of the sales process. During your presentation of the idea, as you attempt contracting, analyze initial and eventual advancement of the deal. Ask yourself, "Have we made progress?"

If you are trying to solve a problem at the contact phase, that's easy enough to measure: you get a response, establish a conference call, or set a meeting within a week or two at the most. If you are unsuccessful for longer than that, no "he's been traveling" excuse can account for a lack of progress. You'll know you've made progress in the conceive level because your team will gain confidence in the right mix of products/services as well as your ROI predictions, and your prospect will not push back on those core assumptions. Often, you'll be invited to present the solution to decision makers. Progress at the convince phase is measured by explicit agreement to key points and a request for an agreement or a discussion about the contracting process. Solving the contract level is the clearest: you get the signature or a time line for when the final deal documents will be obtained.

Find metrics with which you can measure the level of progress. In some sales cultures, potential deals are given a "likely to close" percentage assignment. At Yahoo! we often gave deals a heat score (10 = hot!). Several of my enterprise clients used "days to close" as a metric, with "unknown" as a proxy for an opportunity that's fizzling out or dead. However you do it, the act of measuring gives you a yardstick to judge whether the play possesses incremental value for other situations.

Aside from analyzing progress in the deal process, you should also look for any negative side effects your approach might have triggered.

Did your contact play to reach an influencer or senior decision maker ruffle feathers? Were your attempts to obtain information to conceive the win-win deal seen as intrusive? Was some part of your convince attempt perceived as over the top or silly? Did your contract solution run afoul of the company's common practices or alienate someone in the prospect's legal group?

Too often, our analysis is binary: it worked or it didn't work. But it's really more complicated than that when selling to an enterprise. Sometimes, you win the battle (the deal) but lose the war (the long-term relationship). Your clever hack or persuasive device may have moved things forward, but at a price. Depending on your company's culture, it may be too high a price to pay, even to land a big deal.

Compare your analysis with the notes from the dealstorm meeting(s). Did someone in the room predict this negative by-product? If so, how was her objection defeated? This can reveal errors in mental models (metacognition) that problem owners can have when chasing a deal. That can come in handy later in similar, future situations. In the case of the person who saw the train wreck coming, consider him or her a valuable future resource in a dealstorm.

If the deal is not advancing, confer with your sponsor to gain an understanding of why. You may want to organize what I refer to as a reconvene, which is roughly the same length as the original dealstorm meeting and should include an updated deal brief. In addition to your sponsor, include the same (or some of the same) cast of players you worked with during the verification or prototype feedback stages. In some cases, you might recruit new members based on their expertise or the feedback you've received from the prospect.

In a reconvene, you should once again return to the fishbone diagram to find the root cause of failure in your tested play. For example, if the prospect was not in agreement with your value proposition during a convince attempt, start there and work backward. In this case, you can employ convince-specific categories for the fishbone diagram exercise, such as device (metaphor, illustration), delivery (speaker, style), audience, timing, research (quality, relevance), or competition. Completing an increasingly specific fishbone diagram in a reconvene may produce great insights for the next attempt.

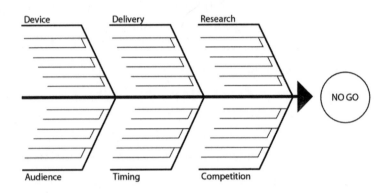

Convince Level

If your proposed solution doesn't get you anywhere, it's time for you to revisit the backup play or other ideas nominated during the meeting or afterward. Analyze whether one of them might break the logjam. Or consider whether a mashup of one or more of those ideas would have produced a better result. Sometimes, your failed attempt gave you much better insights as to the root cause of your deal problem or what the prospect really needs to see, hear, or feel.

In the happy case that your play breaks through the level, you should analyze whether this solution can scale to other sales challenges at your company. When it comes to sales process, the only reason to think outside the box is to make it stronger. If you can take this victory and use insights and ideas from it to help others win, you are truly practicing sales leadership.

This is where your sponsor or fellow account executives can give you feedback. Would your play have worked in a previous situation where a deal was stuck? Are there current opportunities in the pipeline that can put this solution into play? Look for any unique circumstances that contain success only for this prospect, the unique personalities involved, or this particular selling situation.

Compare the new approach with the existing best practice in the sales process and ask yourself, "Have we come up with something new and improved?" In that event, it's important that you or your sponsor escalate the innovative play to senior sales leaders. Prior to inserting it into the sales process or scaling it across the sales group, they may require more instances of the play successfully compressing the sales cycle, increasing the close ratio of prospective deals, or restarting an account relationship.

Over the course of my dealstorm experience, I've seen countless improvements to a company's way of selling and servicing accounts come from the process. At Yahoo!, based on a dealstorm-mined solution and subsequent testing, we changed our prospecting strategy to include partnering with ad agencies when pursuing Fortune 100 companies or advertisers that spent more than one hundred million dollars annually on marketing programs. A software company I worked with changed its method of responding to requests for proposals (RFPs) based on two dealstorms that suggested a better way of pairing features, services, and payment plans to prospective clients. In many situations, dealstorms lead to more effective presentation elements, selling analogies, and relevant case study development for the convince stage. Finally, several media services companies and technology providers have convinced their legal groups or finance directors to reconsider various terms and conditions in their agreements, based on dealstorms that demonstrated that change would accelerate business development without producing more risk. So beyond the process helping on a case-by-case basis, it can greatly strengthen a company's go-to-market selling strategy.

Report

As you execute and analyze any of the next step plays that resulted from your dealstorm, it's important for the sales leader to keep the dealstorming participants in the loop. Don't leave your team hanging. As soon as you've finished your analysis, report the news. In this case, I do like to send a single email to all, letting them know about the implementation and what happened.

If the deal is advancing, note the prospect's initial reactions and signs that the idea eliminated the root cause of the sticking point. If the idea was presented as a proposal or PowerPoint deck, include a link to it on your intranet and in sales force automation. If there's a direct quote from the prospect signaling success, include it in your report. These details give reports a little color.

It's important to give praise to the team for the solution, but be careful not to attribute the ideas to individuals. Remember, there is no lone inventor: genius is a team sport. In the meeting, someone may have nominated an idea, but in almost every situation, the team improved, verified, and worked on it in execution. If you relied on nonteam members in the verification, prototype, or build steps, include them in the distribution list as well and thank them specifically for their time and effort. For even more punch, you can report via video, which can easily be recorded via smartphone, posted online, and embedded into an email without adding to its weight. (See TimSanders.com/DealStorming for a list of current providers.)

If the play worked, and you've determined, along with your sponsor, that it's scalable to other sales challenges, report the results to senior leaders in the sales organization or, depending on the situation, even higher up in the company. After all, the best practices and winning ways in your sales process haven't been around since day one. A thoughtful sales leader (like you) made sure that the right people knew about a new solution to a common problem and then integrated it into onboarding, training, case studies, and escalation procedures. Don't depend on word of mouth or war stories around the sales rally campfire to bring your team's innovation to the rest of the company.

Think about how dated many of your case studies are. In business-to-business sales, where complexity rises every day, rapid problem solving is the ultimate competitive advantage.

But what if the play was a whiff? You still need to report it to the team. They deserve to know how it all turned out. While you report good news quickly, you'd be wise to report neutral or bad news with a little delay while you try to resolve the situation with the backup plan or other alternatives.

Send individual emails to team members and, depending on the level of involvement, others you've resourced in the execution phase of the process. Be honest, but not depressive, in your tone. Link to the presentation elements or proposal just the same; in the case that something was missing, you'll find out through feedback. Indicate when the idea was launched, what initial reactions you observed, and what signals you've received that the sticking point remains. Thank each team member for his or her efforts. Let them know you'll be conferring with your manager, and potentially senior staff, to determine whether the prospective deal or account in crisis warrants more meetings of the team. Invite them to contribute any ideas directly to you that can possibly move things forward. If possible, itemize useful insights or innovations that came out of the dealstorm that might come into play in future sales situations. It's important to make sure everyone knows that her time was well spent, even if the solutions that came out the dealstorm didn't result in immediately moving up a level. In almost every one of my experiences, it *was* time well spent.

Well, you've gone full circle. You've organized, prepared, and led a team through the dealstorm process and shared the results with participants as well as any stakeholders who need to know. If you've clearly leveled up (i.e., the deal's moving forward to signature), congrats! But if it's not so clear, this is where the cyclical nature of this process will work for you. You can repeat it. After you complete the reporting step, you are back to the qualify stage of the dealstorm process, where it's time to determine whether the deal's unstuck, facing a new level of challenge, or dead in the water. Along with your sponsor, you should recalibrate your significance/difficulty formula (from Chapter 4). Is it still a win-win? Based on new insights, how important is the opportunity at this point? Is there a new sticking point that requires the team to reconvene for another round of dealstorming?

At this point, sales leaders should also determine whether the dealstorm process is producing value, either for this particular sales challenge or for future ones. If the meetings are continuing to provide insights and be productive, likely the team should stay together. Most nonsalespeople who join the dealstorm simply want to be kept in the loop and don't expect the team to continue to meet forever.

Don't assume that a singular convene meeting, no matter how wonderful it goes, will be enough to reach the top level. In my experience, the average successful project involves three meetings per sticking point. Sometimes you'll run through the cycle in one convene and two regroups, and in other cases, one convene, one regroup, and, when another sticking point pops up at a higher level, a reconvene.

Because you've been good at reporting progress, your team is likely still at the ready to help you through the next level, or, if you still have lives left in the game, to make another attempt to solve the current level. And along the way, between your meetings and interactions with team members, you've identified some rock stars, some malcontents, and some free riders.

Based on the effectiveness of the dealstorm, the individuals participating, and the blend of personalities in the room, your team may not be the same during the next round of problem solving—and that's OK. Between each season, professional teams draft rookies, trade players, and make roster cuts. That's how they can improve. Collaboration experts recommend periodically infusing new members into the group to revitalize it and spur new thinking. But you don't want the meetings to get bloated, so you'll likely have to make some cuts along the way. As I mentioned earlier, it's natural for meeting size to scale up and down during the process.

For example, to solve the conceive level, you included resources from the product development and finance group. They've been instrumental in putting together a customized solution, then figuring out a pricing model that works for everyone. But now you are on to the convince level, where new skills sets are required. You should replace these participants with leads from marketing and creative design while still retaining team members with a stake in the deal, such as account coordinators.

The transition is pretty easy: the next invitation for a dealstorm meeting need only contain the active team members (including the newbies). Introduce these folks during the meeting, explaining to the rest of the group what they bring to the table. After the meeting, your confirm email only goes out to those who were part of the meeting.

When you choose not to invite a team member to the meeting, send him a quick note to explain why. Typically, it's because the focus of the meeting doesn't require his expertise or that the project has moved in a new direction, requiring new resources. Almost always, he will be fine with not being invited and will appreciate you taking the time to explain.

While you may swap out meeting invitees, anyone who has played on the team should be kept in the loop when it comes time to report on results. All team members deserve to know where the deal is because they've contributed to the cause.

At some point, particularly if you've run through the dealstorming cycle several times without traction, the sales manager and the account executive should huddle and consider the hard question: Is this deal dead?

While the answer is usually subjective, there are four reasons that most sales opportunities should be considered unwinnable. First, the prospect informs the account executive that they do not see a fit for the proposed solution and would prefer not to be contacted again. Second, the sales manager or account exec determines that there is no unique selling proposition, based on prospect feedback. This means that value cannot be convincingly demonstrated after multiple attempts or that a competitor is clearly winning from the prospect's point of view. Third, the sales manager determines that the account executive and dealstorm team's time could be better spent on other opportunities. Finally, the sales manager concludes that continuing to pursue the prospect could damage relationships through annoyance. At larger companies, managers have to consider existing deals with the prospect in other divisions or regions and weigh how continuing the sales process might threaten them.

Even in the case of the seemingly dead deal, there's still a chance for collaboration to make a difference. At Novell, former sales vice president Dan Veitkus loved to bring his dealstorm team back together when he had closed the door on the deal to figure out why they had lost. He would start with a declaration: "I'm making the decision: we've lost the deal. We are walking away. It's up to us to learn a lesson from it for the next time."

Almost every time he made this declaration, he told me, key stakeholders, from account executives to engineers, let go of their egos and talked candidly about what they could have done better. "If I could start over, I'd have brought in a partner to do the integration work instead of asking Larry in engineering," he once heard. Larry replied, "If I knew that this was so important for your presentation, I would have built the wireframe for your final presentation." A remarkable sense of flexibility and cooperation often followed in these candid what-went-wrong review sessions.

In several cases, the team pleaded with Dan for one more crack at the problem, and if appropriate, he relented. "We closed millions of dollars of business that I thought we'd lost, through a newfound willingness to compromise and cooperate. It took a postmortem to bring it out."

While the dealstorm process provides a powerful engine for problem solving, innovation and relationship development provide its fuel. While the process is linear, finding the next play that works isn't so neat. In many situations, your team will need to develop unexpected approaches to the sales challenge that are appropriate to the situation—the essence of creative thinking. In others, you'll need support inside the prospect company or out in the market, which requires networking prowess.

Over the course of the next few chapters, I'll show you how to use role playing to bring out innovation, find outside firepower for your team, and build powerful connections with your team that spur high levels of engagement and courage.

TOOLS FOR INNOVATION

CHAPTER 8

The Hacker, the Chef, and the Artist

I t was my second dealstorm at Yahoo!, and our team was in pursuit of a partnership with one of the world's largest soda brands. We'd spun up a wide range of participants for our meeting, including Bill Miltenberger, who headed up our front page promotions group. He arrived first, just as I was arranging chairs and taping up prelabeled flip charts.

From the moment I arrived at Yahoo!, Bill helped me find my footing and mentored me about the company culture. In the meeting, he continued with his teachings, starting with the following question: "So what role am I playing today?" Without giving it much thought, I replied, "You are a resource." He chuckled. "No, I mean, what's my persona for this meeting? Am I playing detective, safecracker, storyteller or what?"

The deal at the center of this meeting was stuck in the conceive phase, and we were trying to configure a mix of services that would work for this soda company. I had planned on using the Systemic Inventive Thinking template (from Chapter 6) to drive the solution discussion. But that relied solely on the linear way, and, as a creative, Bill wanted to wrap his mind around the problem from a specific point of view.

"What's my motivation?" he continued. It was at that moment I realized that in every problem-solving situation, there are specific mindsets required to unleash truly innovative thinking. While my templates gave the meeting structure, Bill's suggestion to overlay a persona on top of the templates allowed the players to come to the meeting with a distinct perspective. I settled on the idea that all of us would take on the role of chef during the solution discussion, looking for a recipe that we could bake up into a delicious offer.

Bill rolled with it during the meeting, talking about ideas like a chef would, using culinary terms such as "taste profiles," "doneness levels," and even "plating options" to discuss promo campaign ideas. It helped everyone in the room understand how to think about the situation creatively. During the solution discussion, this approach made my SIT template sing as small groups added, multiplied, subtracted, and divided ingredients and processes like Julia Child or Graham Kerr from *The Galloping Gourmet*.

Whether you are the problem owner, sponsor, or a resource, assuming the right persona can improve your creativity in a meeting and enhance your ability to produce work that is unexpected but at the same time appropriate to the situation. While it's impossible to predict what will work, it's not difficult to determine best practices for archetypal characters as they fulfill their roles.

Innovating is not a way of doing things; it's a mode of thinking. As we traverse the sales process, moving through unique levels, we need to know which hat to put on to leverage our imagination and group intelligence. While there are hundreds of potential characters or metaphors we could adopt, I've isolated three that fit the sales process best: the hacker, the chef, and the artist.

To solve the contact level, in most cases it's a matter of finding a new route or taking an unexpected approach. This is the hallmark of the hacker, who seeks out soft spots in the system to exploit.

To conceive the win-win deal, a mashup of ingredients and processes leads to an unbeatable combination. This is what a master chef does, focusing on recipe and execution to produce surprise and delight.

To convince the prospect, abstractions must be reduced into powerful communication devices that produce clarity and desire. That's the essence of the artist, who converts the blank canvas into an evocative picture that trumps a thousand words (or statistics).

The contract level requires something a bit different, as legal and procedural obstacles must be overcome. Often this is achieved by finding a new path to securing a firm commitment from the prospect that doesn't contradict the prospect's internal policies or procedural norms. This requires a hacker mindset and in certain cases, an artist's approach to illustrating why the proposed contractual solution is a win-win.

This chapter will be useful to you regardless of whether you are in a full-blown dealstorm or just problem solving a sales challenge on your own or in tandem with your manager. You'll also find that, in some cases, the three personas can apply to any level when creatively applied.

The Hacker

When the traditional approach fails, a sales hacker explores a new route that produces an unexpected but appropriate solution. Hackers look at the situation from multiple angles and are willing to try new entry points or novel access methods to break through. They ditch the expected and look for blind spots.

Hackers are often thought of as malicious, breaking into computer systems for fun, profit, or revenge. But their method of problem solving has proved useful for organizations of all types. Today the word "hacker" also stands for innovation, particularly in Silicon Valley (Facebook's headquarters, after all, are located at 1 Hacker Way.) Startups pride themselves on finding nontraditional ways to move users or systems from point to point, disrupting their rivals. "White hat" hackers help enterprises find weaknesses in their systems and then boost their cybersecurity. Traditional companies, such as General Electric and Procter & Gamble, host hackathons, where employees explore off the beaten pathways to solve common business problems. Popular authors like Tim Ferriss write about life hacks, inelegant or unorthodox solutions to everyday problems. In all cases, the hacker is driven by intense curiosity and the willingness to explore the unknown until he punches through.

Making the leap to sales, hacking your way past a sticking point might be the order of the day. In the case of the contact level, a prospect's defense against cold calls is formidable these days. Drop-ins are usually prohibited and are blocked by a locked door or a receptionist. Cold calls languish in general voice mailboxes. Direct mail never makes it past the recycle bin. Email addresses are hard to find, and even when they make it to the right recipient, they usually end up in the Junk folder. In all cases, these traditional prospecting tactics are seen as intrusive; thus they are blocked by design, like a body fighting off an illness.

But what if sales could find a hack that converted the cold call into the welcome advance? This is the premise of social selling, a new media–enabled approach to prospecting that leverages a new personal and professional passion: sharing content and experiences. With this passion comes a soft spot: the desire for our updates to be noticed and valued by others.

Recent research by the Edison Group reveals that adults revisit social media networks often to check up on reactions to their updates.[1] When a useful quote, article, or announcement is ignored, it bothers them. In some cases, measuring update engagement can trigger almost half of the visits to these social networks! This creates an opportunity for those stuck in contact to interact with a prospect's updates and postings to build up a warm connection prior to any sales pitch.

Create lists on social networks to follow prospects or influencers and then interact with their most useful or inspirational content. Remember: creative work is not only unexpected, it's appropriate to the situation. You need to be authentic about what you "like" or share. You should recommend only the share-worthy to your connections. Your comments should add to the conversation, not interrupt it. With a little finesse, you'll be surprised how much easier it is to become top of the News Feed and much closer to gaining access to those who matter.

For example, SAP executive Gerry Moran was not responding to a proposal from enterprise social networking service provider People-Browser because he was too swamped to review it. Travis Wallis, vice president of sales at PeopleBrowser, took to LinkedIn, where he engaged with Gerry's posts on an unrelated topic. Gerry noticed his thoughtful comments and immediately scheduled a call with him to discuss the proposal in detail.[2]

LinkedIn also offers a fresh take on networking or referrals. In many cases, you share common contacts with your target prospect, called 2nd- or 3rd-level connections. It appears on the social media site transparently, and dramatically reduces the search time required for you to find a path to the hard-to-contact executive or buyer.

Incorporating social selling into your day-to-day prospecting approach consistently can make a big difference on your total performance. A recent survey revealed that "72.6% of salespeople who incorporated social media into their process outperformed their colleagues."[3] These tech-savvy sellers make contact where the "smile and dial" crowd continues to get voice mail.

At the opposite end of the media spectrum—from digital communications to snail mail—Domino Project promotions director Ishita Gupta found her path to access through a prospect's mail room. She was selling a sponsorship opportunity for a book the company was publishing on how to conduct effective business meetings. There was no precedent for this type of sponsorship, which meant she would need senior support at the prospect company to get the deal done.

There were a limited number of companies that would value such an opportunity enough to pony up the fifty thousand dollars for the program. She and Domino Project founder Seth Godin narrowed down the prospects to Citrix and WebEx, both industry leaders in the meeting provider space. Ishita and Seth didn't have direct contacts at either company, so networking would still be a slow-burn process, and they needed to strike a deal before the book was published just a few months down the line.

They conceived a plan to get a copy of the yet-to-be-published book into the hands of key executives at both companies, each accompanied by a personalized sticky note suggesting that the book would be right up his or her alley. The books would be sent via FedEx (to create urgency) and they'd follow up with a call to see whether the package had arrived and to talk to each decision maker.

Ishita did research identifying the right executives to approach and then went one step further, finding a friend in the mail room at each company. At Citrix, which makes the GoToMeeting virtual conference product, she found Tony, who ran the mail room and was relatively easy to contact. When she called him, she was friendly but went directly to the point: "I've sent an important package to Joe, Stacy, and Mike (executives at Citrix), and I need you to help me get it to them the same day it arrives."

Tony felt empowered by being involved in this mission, and he rose to the occasion, personally delivering the books to each executive's assistant. The books caught the executives' attention—the hand delivery supplemented the book's relevant message and the handwritten sticky note from Ishita and Seth. Within a few days, Ishita held her first conference call with the director of marketing, and when the book was published, Citrix sponsored its launch. Rather than getting stuck at the front door, the Domino team rerouted the pitch path and dramatically shortened the sales cycle.

For many companies, social outreach programs are a soft spot for executives and managers. At chip maker Altera, sales senior vice president Mark Nelson reverse engineered this approach to contacting prospects. "We hold an annual charitable golf tournament, where we choose where the money goes," he told me. "We survey our customers' key outreach programs that are aligned with our social values (education) to make our selection. It creates a unique bond with them, and opens doors to new opportunities."

When used gadget trading exchange startup VenJuvo was trying to make contact with the elusive president of Target's electronics division, it came to consultant John Ruhlin to dealstorm a way in. After doing a little sleuthing, he found out the Target executive was a proud graduate of the University of Minnesota and an active alumni booster. As a person who loved creating one-of-a-kind door openers, John devised a plan to have a 40- by 40-inch, fifty-pound carving made out of a massive piece of cherrywood with the university logo, the gopher mascot, and the school fight song etched on it.

"It was the kind of gift that a ten-million-dollar donor would receive," John told me. The VenJuvo team shipped it to Target headquarters, accompanied by a note asking the retail executive to "carve out some time" to hear about their opportunity. Within two days of receipt, the divisional president's assistant called the sales executive to set up a phone call for the following week.

Using a similar spot-the-affinity approach, a Cox Radio sales team landed a big account with a local attorney who invested heavily in advertising in print publications but wouldn't return their phone calls. Sales manager A.J. Vaughn noticed that the attorney always appeared in his ads donning a flight suit. Via LinkedIn he found out why: the attorney was a former fighter pilot. The sales rep took the lead and found out which plane he had flown and found a die-cast replica of it to drop off at his office, with a short introductory note. He got a meeting right away. The attorney told him, "Well, that's something I never expected!"

When stuck in the contract level, the hacker wins through perceptiveness and timing. When Detroit interactive promotion agency founder Josh Linkner was working on landing a multimillion-dollar deal with food giant ConAgra, he faced a formidable sticking point in getting the final sign-off from its marketing vice president, Michael Bragg. "Something was giving him pause," Josh explained. "We met his criteria, were competent, but he was still in a zone where the deal could go either way."

During this stalled period, both attended the same tech conference and were somehow seated next to each other in first class on the same outbound flight home. Michael's wife was also with him, but her seat was in coach class. As Josh watched the wife kiss her husband goodbye, sigh, and then continue her way to the back of the plane, he felt a pang of empathy for their situation. He, too, traveled often, separated from his wife and family. Even though he had the opportunity to spend four hours with his prospect, he reasoned that he'd already spent a lot of time with him and that a surprising approach to the situation could break the stalemate.

He told the buyer, "Look, I've got a lot of client work to do, and I'd bet you'd like to sit with your wife. Why don't I give her my seat?" Josh got up, collected his bags, and made his way to the back of the plane, where he exchanged boarding passes with the buyer's wife. She began to tear up, saying, "I never get time to spend with him because he travels so much. Thank you!"

His hack was novel as well as compassionate: the no-selling sale. It was a big bet. After all, several hours together in close quarters could have worked wonders for hammering out any final contract points, right? When the plane landed, Josh fired up his BlackBerry to check his messages, only to learn that the buyer had authorized the deal right before the plane took off. This story proves Dale Carnegie's observation that "you accomplish more by developing a sincere interest in others than by trying to get others interested in you."

The Chef

As business is increasingly conducted at the niche, companies or business units are highly specialized so as to be competitive. It takes a network of solution providers to make a customer happy. Cooking up the right deal is often more than looking at your standard menu of products.

During the conceive level, the problem owner needs to act as master chef, combining products, processes, people, or partners to devise a highly relevant menu that delights the prospect. Some recipes will be borrowed, but to create distinction, most chefs must create truly original concoctions.

A chef, first and foremost, is aware of and has access to the right ingredients. For you, those ingredients are solution components that go into the recipes that you combine to conceive the menu (the deal). Your search starts by looking through the lens of your prospect. Review your notes from conversations and, if necessary, conduct additional research to figure out the prospect's pain points. When you made contact, what was the prospect's stated need? What is the implied need? What are the pain points in its business today? What threats exist to its value chain? What trends affect its ability to stay profitable or scalable? These answers will inform the right ingredient mix when trying to conceive the winning deal.

As you organize your team, invite people who know something about the prospect, its industry, and its market. The deal brief should reflect your thoughts on the above questions and invite additional information. The key is to clearly identify the need, which is a function of the prospect's hunger (stated need) and what nourishment it needs (implied need).

Next, check the pantry for relevant ingredients (products and services) that can be brought to the table. Review the current slate that you sell, digging deeper into your company's capabilities, case studies, and even its history. You may have a handful of go-to ingredients to serve up, but to satisfy certain needs, you'll likely have to reach further. This requires an intense curiosity on your part, driven far beyond what sells the most or is easiest to deliver.

At leasing company Regus, dealstorming sessions led agents to combine products in order to satisfy the total needs of their customers, locking out competitors from chipping away at their "value gaps." One of their most popular products is a mailing address stop and reception service, perfect for a virtual office. Many prospects also need occasional office space to meet with clients but cannot afford to lease a dedicated space. Today, Regus sales reps combine the low-cost Office Anywhere membership with the address stop service to give prospects both solutions within budget, just one example of ingredient combining that sated prospects' needs.

Advertising sales veteran Vince Thompson found a way to introduce an exciting ingredient into his larger marketing solutions. He brings in a third-party research group to conduct postcampaign analysis and deliver a case study white paper to the client. This component adds only thirty thousand dollars to a multimillion-dollar campaign, "but has the effect of adding a pinch of truffles to the final product," he says. "For the marketer, he not only receives an ad campaign, he now has a deliverable he can share internally or from the podium at a trade conference."

This twist can be used in other B2B sales, where third-party analysis can become a proof point, talking document, or compliance device. For example, if you are selling a multimillion-dollar water pump equipment system, add postinstallation environmental research to deliver added value with a small incremental addition to the sale.

Here's another technique borrowed from chefs. Skillsoft's Danielle Saurer manages channel partnerships with resellers in order to scale the company's distribution of their training solutions. When she took over this role in 2012, she focused on expanding Skillsoft's relationship with a leading provider of payroll and benefits services. The provider supplies a technology platform and works with partners such as Skillsoft to provide courseware or training content in order to provide a complete HR solution.

Sales reps sold Skillsoft on a discovery basis: when they spotted a need for training solutions, they'd add them to the proposal. The problem was that the content sale often held up the platform sale, which was more important—and profitable—to the partner. Danielle and her team organized a dealstorm to find a way to reduce the friction their products created and came up with a tasty plan, which they termed "folding in."

"Instead of being an add-on, we found a way to become an extension of their platform," she explained. This involved a lot of internal negotiating at Skillsoft on her part, as folding their services into the platform required working outside of their normal pricing model. Her manager, serving as the team's sponsor, helped get this new approach approved based on the scale it brought Skillsoft and the likelihood that it would work for other dormant or tepid selling partners. Folding in this ingredient, instead of serving it as a side dish, was the winning touch for prospects who wanted a single serving of product offering. Resale of Skillsoft products ramped up exponentially in just a few years.

If you work at a large enterprise with multiple strategic business units, you may need to expand your concept of the cupboard to include offerings that may not be part of your compensation plan or quota. This may involve including other players who have not historically played nice with you in dealing with a common customer. But if you are stuck in a must-win deal, and you really want to solve the problem, you'll have to transcend your personal needs and fears.

This is what Glen Rosen and his team did at SunGard, a software company focused on the financial services industry. He's one of the company's most successful account executives because of his flexibility when it comes to solving the entire customer's problem. "He's commercially creative in finding the win-win," said his manager, Anthony LoPresti. "He knows that sometimes you've got to go against the grain."

When Glen pursued a strategic relationship with a leading global bank, few thought he could win. When SunGard received the RFP, it was clear that his prospect was looking for a highly customized solution and had likely done a lot of their own research already, talking themselves into looking for a partner that would create a one-of-a-kind package. SunGard, however, seeks to avoid customization, as it is not scalable and doesn't provide the same predictable level of service that their standard products do.

Like an innovative chef, Glen first sought to guide their taste buds in a different direction. By studying his competitor's approach in building a custom solution, he saw a steep learning curve ahead for his prospect. He helped his contacts understand that what they needed was a whole solution made of the right set of tried-and-true standard products.

But to deliver the whole package, he needed to reach across SunGard, bringing in the consulting group to round out his recipe with software integration services. When doing this type of cross-departmental problem solving, it's easy to find yourself with too many cooks in the kitchen, actually making the experience more complicated for the buyer. "So he brought integration solutions in at the end of the process, where it could stand alone," explained his manager,

Anthony. "It made the deal in the end." It was the cherry on top of the cake.

In some situations, the dealstorm team must consider whether an outside partner should be added to the recipe. Software and technology providers often bring in systems integrators to complete the offering. Media companies add targeting software providers or campaign reporting agencies to their proposals to finish the package. In most cases, there's little downside unless the outsider fails to do its job.

Sometimes to complete the package, you have to bring in a partner who is also a competitor. When LG Architects pursued a contract to provide design services for the renovation of the Oakey Campus for Opportunity Village, cofounder Craig Galati knew he would need to bring in outside help. This facility provides educational services for Las Vegas residents with intellectual and learning disabilities. "We needed to better understand the perspective of those with this disability," he told me. So they reached out to Baltimore-based architect Jane Rohde, whom they knew from a previous project where she was brought in to peer review their work. She had deep experience in designing for the disabled and was more than eager to contribute to both the sales process and the project, if won.

"Her understanding of the client's design needs was amazing," he said. "Part of her expertise is her knowledge about the role that color, patterns, and texture play in the well-being of the intellectually disabled. She also understood the unique needs of the staff for such a facility, and what they'd need to better do their job." Jane contributed to the project proposal and participated in the final presentation to Opportunity Village leaders, which resulted in winning a contract. By combining their architectural expertise and knowledge of the community with Jane Rohde's subject-matter savvy, LG Architects found the perfect recipe to design a solution from the end user's point of view.

While architects are known for sharing projects with peers when it makes sense, bringing competitors into the deal process can open the door to losing the business. This is where things can get complicated. Competitors usually have different corporate values, and in many cases they would like to take your spot in the kitchen. It's important to figure out which ones can be trusted, based on their desire to set aside the past in order to serve the client in the future. When blending them into the mix, you need to constantly check on how things are coming together and be willing to make adjustments on the fly.

I had to do this while working as a sales rep at Broadcast.com in 2001. My goal was to satisfy my most demanding customer, Victoria's Secret. We had hosted its fashion show webcast the year before, which succeeded at gaining a lot attention for their new website launch, but the webcast ultimately crashed as a result of the millions of users who logged in simultaneously. This time, the client wanted the event to go off without a hitch, as the desired outcome was stimulating e-commerce, not just raising the buzz factor.

After conferring with our CEO, Mark Cuban, it became clear we couldn't single-handedly stream the client's event to the millions who would likely sign on. So I searched for cohosts we could work with to create a redundant network for the client. In this case, I needed to bring more bandwidth, more equipment, and even a few of our competitors into the streaming services space to win the client. It was risky business, but we could not fail again.

There were many personality profiles involved, and our competitors had direct access to our client, which is always scary. In this experience, I learned the importance of being a client-focused leader throughout the process, relegating my partner to sous chef or server. I ran the meetings, issued the reports, and wasn't afraid to call down anyone stepping outside his station. By keeping the client's needs at the center of the table, I was able to marshal the authority to call myself top chef.

This is an important point to keep in mind any time you are mashing up outside parties to create your solution: the problem owner should never cede control of the kitchen.

The Artist

"Show me, don't tell me" is one of the best pieces of sales effectiveness advice I've received. The late Stanley Marcus Jr., former CEO of Neiman Marcus department stores, shared this nugget during a lunch meeting in 1999.

I was telling him how video streaming, e-commerce, and Internet advertising all came together to create "the new economy" of retail. For forty-five minutes, I talked about Moore's Law, quoted statistics about user adoption, and retold Mark Cuban's story about how our company, Broadcast.com, was founded. Finally, Mr. Marcus slid his journal and Cross pen across the table and asked me to draw him a picture of "how this ecosystem worked." I tried telling him that I wasn't artistically inclined. He wasn't having it.

"The painter doesn't talk about the countryside. He shows us," he said. "The photographer doesn't have to describe the feelings of her subject. She shows us the picture. Reduce the abstraction so I can grasp this new future you are so excited about."

His request made me realize that people resist facts and figures but lean into illustrations and images. We use an entirely different part of our brains, which enables us to deeply understand complex ideas in a moment. Art convinces in the moment and, better, continues to convey meaning when shared, even absent the presence of the artist or curator. This is why the artist persona is an important part of solving the convince level of the sale.

Just a few years after my lunch with Mr. Marcus, this came into play during one of our darkest moments at Yahoo!. By early 2001, the dot-com bubble was bursting, likely popped by financial analysts like

Holly Becker, of Lehman Brothers, who declared, "Banner ads don't produce value because no one clicks on them." The ad agencies that represent major brands like Nike, Procter & Gamble, and Sony responded with a new business model for us: pay per click.

At the time, we sold advertising mostly on the basis of the number of impressions we served. In other words, we sold our audience's attention. But the agencies wanted to buy traffic to their customer's websites, even though most of their clients sold through physical retail channels. If we didn't overcome this challenge, our net sales would likely drop by 80% or more. Talk about a crisis!

We organized a set of dealstorm meetings that included account executives, marketing directors, brand researchers, agency partners, and sales operations managers. As we compared notes, we gathered evidence that the ads we delivered to our users *did* make an impression, driving purchase intent or brand awareness, even if they never clicked on them for "more information." We thought, *Eureka! We have the proof!*

I attended multiple meetings between our sales team and ad agency account planners, where our statistics fell on deaf ears. Our Excel spreadsheets on brand-awareness lift were met with blank stares. While they couldn't deny our findings, they couldn't get past the new paradigm: measurable results that they could see.

During our next dealstorm, it hit me: "Show them, don't tell them." We collectively came up with a way to powerfully illustrate our total value proposition to the ad agency account planners, using a graphic we called "The Iceberg." It combined an image with the numbers. The ice above the waterline represented the ad interactions or clicks. Everything below the waterline represented the views and the brand impressions. We dotted the image with various statistics, creating an infographic of sorts.

Immediately, we saw results in the field. One agency head clapped his hands and said, "That's exactly what we needed." It turns out that, in most cases, they were also trying to convince their clients that there was more value to banner ads than meets the eye, but our spreadsheets and bullet points weren't coming across. In this case, our team thought like artists, leveraging visual imagery to get over the hump. Thinking like an artist and producing visual tools like this arms prospects with something they can use to sell you forward to people you'll never get a chance to pitch directly.

CareerBuilder's Alyssa DeMattos used artistry to prevent a sticking point from raising its ugly head. Earlier, I told you about how she was faced with the challenge of producing a prototype for Allegis, so they could "see what they were buying." While she succeeded at getting engineers to build a functional version of the career site, according to Alyssa, "It was bare bones, with no design wow at all."

Jay, head of marketing at the Aerotek division, was a key influencer attending the finals presentation in Baltimore, where the prototype would be revealed. "He will tell you that he has the attention of a goldfish," Alyssa said. "If he didn't like the look of it, he wouldn't get why we were capable of building something they could be proud of."

Realizing this, she rallied for internal resources from the IT group to "pretty it up and make it look more finished." They pushed back; they had given up precious time on the build and needed to get back to their projects. "These superficial things aren't important. It's the technology," was their reply to her. While her persistence got some attention to its look and feel, by the time of the big meeting she knew it wouldn't be up to Allegis design standards.

She and her team came up with an idea for setting expectations with a strong visual analogy. The first slide of her presentation flashed a picture of actor Scarlett Johansson fetching coffee in her workout clothes, without any makeup on. "Her look here is like the prototype we are about to demo for you. Good bone structure, but not a finished product." Then, Alyssa clicked to the next slide, which featured another photo of Johansson, in this case walking the red carpet at the Oscars, looking like a million bucks.

"We'll let you choose the makeup and clothes" for the final product, she explained. The analogy clicked with Jay from Aerotek as well as everyone else in the room. Later, when business and technology managers through Allegis were shown the "down and dirty" demo, whenever they'd sniff about its look and feel, the ScarJo before-and-after device was parroted from the meeting: "The bones are great here; we'll dress it up for the market!"

This is the value of visually based analogy: it helps others tell it forward. This is especially valuable when there are multiple influencers weighing in on the sale. To solve a price-to-value sales challenge, Regus employed a similar comparison. Regus offers office space with multiple amenities, usually in a tony shopping center in an upscale neighborhood. Their monthly rents are the highest in most of their markets, reflecting the added value they offer. When prospects visit, the features and the buzz around the offices wow them. But later, when they tell their associates about it, they get feedback that they are paying too much per square foot.

In the Denver office, leasing agent Mike Smith came up with a creative solution: a tale of two vehicles. Now, when he hears this common objection, he tells prospects to compare a cargo van with a BMW X5 SUV. The former will deliver the lowest price per square foot of cargo, but the latter offers the ultimate driving experience.

"It's a choice you make, based on your personal tastes and needs," he explains. He then points to a poster board in his office that compares the two vehicles. This usually does the trick, not only quelling any concerns expressed by the prospects, but also equipping them with a comeback when a helpful friend rattles off a cheaper office quote he's read about in the paper.

For many companies, the challenge is to explain exactly what they do for companies, whether in the contact or convince levels. This is what Brett Tabano faced at Videology, a marketing solutions company focused on helping marketers efficiently and effectively place video advertising on broadcast networks and websites. Absent a clear under-standing of the value-add in terms of Videology's technology, partner-ships, and back-end measurement, they either can't get in the door or get lumped in with the heavily commoditized "advertising networks," which aggregated media inventory from publishers and then sold it on price.

During a recruiting interview, Tabano stumbled across a metaphor that worked with an engineer candidate: the mall. "You go there because they are customized to have everything you need," he explained. "There are bookend department stores, like Macy's and Bloomingdale's. Then there are the specialty stores in between. We have built the mall on our platform and aggregated all the stores to make it work for advertisers as well as the media publishers they buy from." The engineer got it right away, and Brett set out to create a slide image to display it for future pitches.

As he designed it, he anchored his video advertising "mall" with audience supply and audience demand on either end. Publishers entered the mall through audience supply, and marketers (their cus-tomers) entered through audience demand. Specialty stores on the mall's interior included partners such as Nielsen, which supplied audi-ence data and online campaign ratings (OCR) that verified that the ads were served. Creative services, from copywriting to digital enhancement, dotted the "food court," rounding out the offering for marketers as well as their publisher suppliers who provided the ad inventory. The "Video Ad Mall" slide dramatically shortened the time it took to answer the otherwise vexing question, "What exactly does Videology do?" It also positioned Videology as a platform provider and not just an ad aggregator.

Tip: If you work at a company with a complex business concept, confer with a recruiter from human resources to find out what analogy she uses to describe the company to candidates. He or she has likely had to go through the drill of selling your company daily and may have the image, illustration, or metaphor that'll help you cut through the fog during your next big meeting.

For ChangeLabs founder Peter Sheahan, the artist persona manifests itself in the sketches he uses to persuade prospects to sign on with his training company. "The magic moment in my presentation is when I ask the prospect permission to use their whiteboard," he explained to me. "I draw a diagram of their market space, their business drivers, and where our training programs fit in. If the prospect ever asks for the magic marker to add to it, my closing ratio is north of eighty percent." Today, he integrates chalk talk into his conference presentations, dramatically improving his audience's understanding of the concepts that he's sharing.

Jay Milligan, Stewart Title's chief enterprise sales officer, loves to use sketching instead of PowerPoint presentations. "When I'm having a meeting with C-suiters, I like to have it in a conference room with whiteboards," he told me. "I start with a series of questions as part of the discovery phase; then, based on my notes, I get up and create a process flow chart, inserting where we can add value." Then he puts one sheet in front of them that contains key facts or figures. He developed this tactic during his time selling advisory services for Deloitte.

"Drawing out the world for them creates a high level of engagement," he said, "but you need to do your homework and strategize with your team how that world may look." In other words, during the dealstorm meetings, part of the solution discussion can be a strategy session for how the sketching process might play out. "The more familiar and credible your diagram or chart is to them, the more likely they are to engage with you on the whiteboard. And their level of interaction signals the likelihood of them doing business with you," he concluded.

I've employed this tactic with several of my dealstorm clients, and often someone in the room will proclaim, "I'm not artistically inclined." I usually respond by having him draw a simple circle, box, and line drawing on a piece of paper to diagram his department's structure or how various units at the company connect. It's usually quite passable as an expression tool, proving that you don't have to be Rembrandt to use artistry in business. Just be prepared. For a good primer on how to harness your sketching and drawing powers, read *The Doodle Revolution* by Sunni Brown.

While images or sketches can persuade or engage, sight, sound, and motion can pull at heartstrings and change minds. At Prudential Retirement's enterprise division, which sells technology solutions such as record keeping and employee engagement, they've combined those forces to generate millions of dollars of new business.

Michael Domingos leads the company's large market sales group, which pursues megadeals through a dealstorming process with a group they refer to as the SEALs team (inspired by Navy SEAL teams). They engage subject matter experts, account executives, marketing leads, and analysts to plan their "finals" presentations with qualified prospects. During one SEAL meeting in 2013, an account executive suggested that they kick off their pitch by showing a video of the nationally televised commercial "Age Stickers," featuring psychologist Dan Gilbert.

The commercial highlights a forty-foot-high, 1,100-square-foot wall erected in a park in Austin, Texas. Every ten feet, there is a sign with an age on it, from 60 to 110 years old. Hundreds of people were given stickers to place along the wall, signifying the oldest person they've known. Not surprisingly, most stickers were placed beyond the 60-year sign, some as far out as 109 years old. This visually reinforced the need for retirement planning that lasted a person's whole life. (See it at http://ispot.tv/a/7IhP.)

A creative marketing manager in the meeting added to the plan, suggesting they replicate the exercise during the pitch, erecting a two-by-three-foot wall on the conference table, with ages 60 through 110 evenly spaced on it. The idea was to show the video, then put the question "Who is the oldest person you know?" out to everyone.

Because the pitches included multiple presenters, the "dot wall" was used as a transition piece. A presenter would check in by placing a dot on the wall, say, above the ninety mark, and say, "My Auntie Lane is ninety-three and still going strong," and then begin his presentation. An account coordinator suggested that they extend this offering to the retirement committee members attending the meeting "so they could get in on the action." By the end of their presentations, prospects were so engaged that when asked to place their dots on the wall and tell their stories, they almost always obliged. The exercise had a visceral impact on them, as it humanized retirement and underscored how much of a gap many people had between their retirement plans and life expectancy.

"When everyone on the retirement committee places dots on the wall, we win the deal almost every time," Michael said. After several successful executions of the "dot wall" approach, he shared it with other mangers during a weekly "best practices" conference call. Today, it's a go-to component for sales executives at all levels of the enterprise.

Each persona offers members on the dealstorm team a creative framework for solution finding at each level of the sale. The key is to know which persona is right for the task. Assume the hacker mentality when an unexpected approach is required to move the sales process forward. Adopt the chef's mindset when a multi-ingredient approach is required to satisfy the prospect's hunger for value, clarity, or security. Take the artist's way when an improved device is required to illustrate a complex concept or to support a contentious claim.

While I've suggested the use of one persona at a time, there are situations where combining them can produce a more powerful result.

A technology services company I consulted with was attempting to land a beachhead deal with a federal agency to host all of their data in the cloud. The value proposition was twofold: save money and space because the agency would no longer need to maintain and store dozens of computer servers. The prospect was on the fence, mainly because it would be a radical departure from its method of managing its technology on premises.

The dealstorm team initially approached the problem as artists, looking for an illustration that could bring the prospect over to their side. During one of the meetings with the prospect at headquarters outside Washington, DC, the sales reps overheard two of the agency managers talking about their train rides in that day, commenting on how glad they were that they didn't have to own a car anymore. Based on this observation, the dealstormers built an analogy to explain cloud efficiency. Cloud computing, they posited, is the mass transit of the information highway. It offers organizations the opportunity to have all the tech power they need without the cost and hassle factor of owning equipment. The team discussed building graphics for their next presentation illustrating the historical savings of mass transit, then another to mirror the image, recounting the benefits of hosting in the cloud.

Knowing that they still needed to overcome the prospect's security concerns, the team adopted the chef's mindset, looking for an analogy that would do the trick. One of the finance members of the group described a recent startup competition he'd attended, where founders explained their companies by mashing up known entities with markets, calling themselves "the Airbnb, for pets!" or "John Deere meets Uber!" He explained that this approach resonated with investors because the reference to an established service served as a heuristic for dependability.

After twenty minutes of ideation, the group landed on a recipe for success: *We are like DC Metro meets ADT Security Systems!* Their marketing group created a single PowerPoint slide illustrating this concept, documenting DC Metro's cost savings for commuters and ADT's track record of monitoring properties of all types. This slide successfully helped their prospects overcome their fears and then easily explain this to other influencers at the agency.

The whole point of taking on a persona is to find a better lens through which to see the problem and then tweak it to focus in on the winning next play. Too often we see the world through our day-to-day experiences or based on our role at work. By adopting a new point of view, you open up possibilities for creativity in everyone on the dealstorm team. As Alan Kay, the inventor of the computer graphical interface, often said, "A change in perspective is worth 80 IQ points."[4]

CHAPTER 9

With a Little Help from Your Friends

W hen Condé Nast CEO Chuck Townsend presented John Livesay with the Salesperson of the Year award in 2012, he told him, "This is a big deal!" Never before had a *W* magazine rep won this award; it was usually given to someone at *GQ*, *Vanity Fair*, or *Architectural Digest*. Those publications had market power that yielded epic deals.

John won because he accomplished something remarkable: he resurrected the mega Guess account and then closed an exclusive anniversary cocelebration deal with them, triggering national fashion trade coverage that underscored the enduring relevance of print advertising. He solved a host of psychological, creative, and financial problems along the way, with the help of a wide team that included members from marketing, public relations, event planning, print production, and a most unlikely sales collaborator, editorial.

Dozens of meetings, mock-ups, and conference calls added up to a series of innovative moves, but in the end, the dealstorm team needed outside help to win. "We made this happen with a little help from our friend Andrea Chao, the advertising director at Guess," John said.

In May 2011, John was rehired at *W* to bring back the Guess account after being let go in a consultant-ordered reorganization of the magazine a year earlier. After being one of *W*'s biggest clients for decades, Guess CEO Paul Marciano pulled all the company's ads after the magazine featured a nude Kim Kardashian on the cover of the November 2010 issue. Paul fired off a letter to the magazine's editor-in-chief and CEO, declaring that "*W* no longer fit the Guess brand" and that the two companies would no longer be marketing partners. Executives at *W* were thunderstruck by this development because Guess was one of their most important relationships.

John's first plan of action was to give Paul a month or so to cool off before approaching him about renewing their relationship. In the meantime, he reengaged with Andrea Chao, who liked him and valued *W* as a strong platform for marketing Guess products. "She was sad to see our relationship severed," said John. "In Italy, *W* is a leading publication. This is a market where Guess is even more revered than Prada." Andrea knew that getting back into business with *W* was important to their global brand equity; it was a matter of finding a starting point, which she believed John could provide.

Andrea had a lot of influence with Paul Marciano, Guess's CEO. He'd recruited her away from the prestigious Lipman ad agency in New York City, which represented brands he deeply admired. She worked directly with him in his capacity as the company's chief creative officer. He appreciated her insights about fashion trends as well as business development. She was also well connected throughout the company, with relationships spanning from retail to public relations.

In their first meeting after John's return to *W*, he told her, "We are going to win your business back. But in the meantime, I'm going to treat you like our best client." He sent her advance copies of issues. When *W* published editorials featuring models who were under contract with Guess, the credits would indicate this in the magazine; traditionally, such a credit was given only to active advertisers. He also gave Andrea research on fashion industry trends and market forecasts.

During their regular lunch meetings, he tried to gain a better understanding of why the relationship had been severed. "I am surprised by Paul's reaction to the Kardashian issue," John told her. "Sexuality has always been a part of Guess's marketing." There was more to the story, Andrea replied.

In March 2010, *W*'s longtime editor-in-chief, Patrick McCarthy, resigned under pressure as a result of an internal struggle at the magazine. He and Paul were good friends, and there was resentment that he had been forced out. Paul didn't know the new editor, Stefano Tonchi, at all. Because they had no distinct relationship, the situation essentially created a tinderbox in which the account could be blown up with a spark. The controversial Kardashian issue provided the friction.

Based on this insight, John set out a plan of action with Andrea. Stefano had a love for fine wine, and Paul had a wine cellar in his Bel-Air home that was "to die for." Stefano and Paul were both photography enthusiasts. If they hung out, John reasoned, they'd likely find common ground. They would arrange a sit-down between Paul and Stefano so that they could properly meet and hopefully bond over their shared interests.

The key was to make the meeting happen, which was difficult given Paul's hard feelings over McCarthy's ouster and Stefano's embarrassment over Paul's letter to *W*'s CEO criticizing his editorial taste. Finally, John's dealstorming sponsor, the associate publisher, persuaded her boss to coax Stefano into meeting with him when he next visited Los Angeles.

Stefano reluctantly agreed, knowing it was important to the magazine and that he wasn't expected to sell anything, just talk about creative interests. Paul's interest in meeting him was tepid, however, so there was nothing triggering the parlay. Several weeks went by, and no meeting was scheduled.

Around that time, John Livesay found out that one of Stefano's best friends was coming out with a high-profile coffee table photography book. He asked his associate publisher to request an advance copy of the book for Paul, along with a note from Stefano.

Andrea agreed to hand deliver the book to Paul when they had their next standing Saturday-morning briefing. When she delivered it, she reiterated how much he'd likely have in common with Stefano and that it would be a good use of his time to learn about new photographers and up-and-coming models.

A few days later, Paul told his assistant to find a spot on his calendar for a meeting with Stefano at his house. Prior to them getting together, John briefed Stefano on Paul's background and interests, using his sponsor as a proxy because sales never directly worked with editorial. Andrea created a brief for Paul, bringing him up to speed on Stefano's background as well as some upcoming photo shoots he was attending.

When the two of them got together, they compared creative notes, talked trends, and generally hit it off thanks to their shared interests. Stefano shared the perspective that drove his editorial direction; Paul shared his vision for the Guess brand. Paul came to believe that the *W* editorial strategy would actually be aligned with his Guess brand concept over the next few years.

Within a month, Andrea got the news: the relationship with *W* magazine was back on! However, the deal would only be at half the volume of the initial arrangement because Guess was now committed to other magazines for ad programs.

During a subsequent dealstorm, a marketing researcher revealed to John that Guess was celebrating its thirtieth anniversary that falls at the same time that *W* was celebrating its fortieth. The team devised a plan to produce a special Guess anniversary publication that would be bundled with its own anniversary edition and sent out to *W*'s subscribers. This "onsert" (sized the same as the magazine it accompanies) would feature Guess models who had graced the cover of *W* over the years.

At their next lunch meeting, John asked Andrea, "What is your current wow project?" She told him she was planning something to commemorate the brand's thirtieth year. He told her about *W*'s upcoming anniversary, then struck with the proposal for the onsert. He pointed out how the two companies often intersected around models, such as Drew Barrymore, and how the special publication would create a halo effect for both brands.

She liked the idea and added that the magazine launch could be accompanied by an event in Los Angeles, a cocelebration of the two brand's milestones. John's team later suggested the event could display blow-ups of the model photos from the onsert on the walls, making it a showing as well as a party. Models and actors would be invited to the launch, along with key fashion reporters and bloggers.

The big problem was that this was a million-dollar idea, and Andrea didn't have the budget for it. She rolled up her sleeves and went to work inside Guess, drumming up a return-on-investment formula based on the publicity the event would generate and the resulting bump it could have on the stock price—always a driver for Paul. Still, even though she built a strong case for the program, only half the money was committed.

When she delivered the news to John, he replied, "Hey, this cocelebration is a game changer. Let's not let this idea die on price." Andrea countered with a modified proposal. "What if we just did a regional drop, including New York City and Los Angeles?" she said. "That would still get my publicity, and our key markets would love it." She revealed to him exactly how much money she could spend, and he took the number back to corporate to make his case.

At first, his management worried that half of the deal wasn't enough to justify all the heavy lifting that went into producing the onsert and the event. His team did its homework, creating a profit and loss statement that showed it was still a profitable idea, and the program was approved.

The event, dubbed "Iconic & Unforgettable: Guess and *W*," was a smashing success. The press, entertainment community, and brass from both companies all came together in celebration. It was a mammoth win for *W* magazine, as they were the exclusive partner with Guess for their anniversary promotion. When Condé Nast executives huddled to pick their top salesperson for 2012, it was a no-brainer: John Livesay was the rock star of the conglomerate.

After receiving the award in New York City, John stepped out of the ballroom and called his superfriend Andrea Chao to share the good news. She was thrilled for him. It wasn't just a win for John, she said, "It was a win for everybody, me included. Paul still keeps stacks of the special onsert here in the lobby." That was her trophy, proudly displayed to any visitor to Guess headquarters.

Inside Champions

John's success story underscores the importance of having an inside champion, classically defined as "a person who takes a voluntary interest in the adoption, implementation and success of a cause or product."[1] Your champion guides you through the treacherous sales process. He is willing to inform you when roadblocks pop up, will advocate your product, and, if required, fight on your behalf.

At every level of the sale, a superfriend inside the prospect company can elevate you.

Corporate Executive Board (CEB) refers to the most effective inside champions as mobilizers and in 2014 conducted vast research regarding their importance. "Because a supplier has limited access to buying group members during the early stages of the process, it needs the active help of an advocate inside the customer organization," authors Karl Schmidt, Brent Adamson, and Anna Bird wrote in the *Harvard Business Review*.[2] These mobilizers drive change inside their organizations by helping to create consensus among stakeholders with diverse agendas. They get you and your offer in front of influencers and decision makers by vouching for you and opening doors. Later in the process, they marshal support for your company and drive others to action.

Too often, your team takes an insular view about what solution you should sell or what problem you can solve, whereas an insider champion can provide a fuller picture. Software sales veteran Dan Veitkus puts it this way: "Your insider advocate can confirm or deny your pain assessment. In a lot of cases, they'll take you behind the firewall, where the private pain lives. They'll reveal the real problem they are willing to invest in, yet don't want to admit to you because they know you'll leverage it to create urgency or a price premium."

As I documented in the first chapter, the number of influencers weighing in on a deal is increasing exponentially. You'll never get a chance to pitch them all, and certainly you won't be invited to the meetings where the decisions are hammered out. This is where your champion makes her biggest difference to the outcome.

In enterprise sales, Steve Kaplan is somewhat of a legend. He and his teams have sold marketing solutions, enterprise services, industrial equipment, and consulting services to half of the Fortune 500. His victories led him to pen a bestselling book on sales, *Bagging the Elephant*. He, too, believes in the power of internal champions. "Your inside champion fights for your deal behind closed doors," he told me. "They'll overcome objections you'll never hear about." I asked him to expand on his experience.

"About three out of four teams that lose the deal never know why," he explained. "You aren't in the room, and you'll never hear the dirty laundry that makes a big difference on the final outcome. Your champion will throw it on the competition, or find some way to get you over the pile."

Steve isn't suggesting that having one champion is all you need to win a deal. He's always vowed to rep the best products and services because that's key to long-term relationships. "But with an inside champ," he says, "you can still win even when your competitor is ten percent better or twenty percent cheaper."

In some cases, a champion can serve as informant, especially when a competitor is about to leapfrog you. Software industry sales veteran Rizan Flenner was almost to the finish line on a multimillion-dollar sale when he received a text message from his inside champion, the VP of operations. "In board meeting right now. Other members leaning towards your competition, who says it can be done for less money. They are coming in 1 hr to present. Ideas?"

Rizan sprang to action, gathering his marketing team and reviewing everything they knew about their competitors. He sent back his champion with two key questions that tripped up the competition during their presentation, leading him to deal victory.[3]

Finding this superfriend is not a direct process like cold calling. You don't prospect for a champion. You discover a good candidate and then develop her desire to help as well as her ability to effectively advocate your cause. Steve Kaplan recommends looking for a lateral match, someone who's relatively equal in stature to you. This is contrary to the make-a-friend-with-the-CEO approach taught by most sales gurus. "A matching-rank relationship is credible," he explains. "He or she's a lot more likely to have common ground with you, which serves as the relationship piece of the puzzle."

It's important that you don't look for the first friendly face; otherwise, you'll make some account friends who can't really help you. They might be encouraging, but your deal will not advance. Silicon Valley startup adviser Paul Weinstein coaches sales leaders on how to navigate the complexity of selling technology to big organizations. He identifies the four traits that make champions as valuable as they are: "credibility, connections, company intelligence, and motivation."[4]

But what does it take to motivate the champion to be more loyal to you than his own organization? After all, giving you inside information or fighting for you comes with risk. Why would she do that? CEB researchers suggest that the best champions initially step up for you because they believe your company can add business value to their organization.[5] That's why they help you with introductions and assist your diagnostic efforts.

If an account contact relates to you or likes you, you'll get some coaching from him on the sale. But don't kid yourself; he may like you, but he likes his employer, job security, and family a lot more. This is why you need to look deeper to find those triggers that convert a friend to a champion. CEB found that for mobilizers, "factors such as whether a solution could advance a person's career or help him be seen as a better leader were five times as potent as the offering's business value—things like superior product features, likely impact on business outcomes, or return on investment." Wow, that's a whole lot of motivation! This suggests seeking out those who are seeking more credibility or authority. If you can offer them benefits like this, you're more likely to find a champion willing to bear some risk for you down the line. (Note: Those who are self-promotional more than enterprise focused are often seen as less credible to their colleagues, so pick your aspiring leader carefully.)

Look for signs of engagement as you conduct your early-stage capabilities presentations in front of large account prospect groups. As you roll out key benefits, you'll see some people yawn and others respond with enthusiasm. The latter group offers you a field of potential champions.

This was a lesson learned when I was selling a webcasting solution to Victoria's Secret in 1998. My first pitch meeting at their headquarters in Columbus, Ohio, was attended by my primary contact, who managed their online business, along with six corporate executives. One of them was Tim Plzak, the chief technology officer for their parent company, The Limited. He ended up becoming my champion.

Victoria's Secret was looking to promote the launch of their website, and we had agreed that their upcoming fashion show was a good candidate for an online broadcast event. After I outlined our video streaming and promotional capabilities, I rolled out a return-on-investment strategy that I thought would appeal to the finance executives in the room.

As part of the event registration, we would capture email addresses of the viewers and give them a chance to opt out of receiving the Victoria's Secret catalog by mail, receiving it via email instead, as a PDF file. No printing or mailing costs necessary, I emphasized. I predicted that we could easily convert a quarter million people initially, which could lead to a tipping point that could change their model and save millions of dollars over the next few years.

Tim Plzak lit up like a Christmas tree when I showed him the slide with my predictions about e-adoption by Victoria's Secret's customer base. His broad smile gave away his enthusiasm for my proposed solution. For him, a jump in digital catalog subscriptions would generate a dramatic boost to his group's power base, which he believed was the future of the company. The print catalog lived in business operations and was both the cash cow and largest expense of the company. His technology group managed store operations, telecommunications at corporate, digital marketing, and the fledgling website. If Victoria's Secret went more digital, CTO world would be even more powerful.

For the next few years, Tim was my confidante, coach, and networking buddy at the company. When our event crashed in '98, he explained to everyone inside The Limited why that was "a healthy problem, and a learning experience." He wrangled partners and resources to help us succeed the second time that we broadcast their fashion show, including giving us proprietary access to their enterprise technology map. He even introduced me to the marketing director at sister company Lane Bryant, which led to a webcast event the next year. With each new deal, technology and, more specifically, his group gained power at The Limited.

The takeaway from this example is that you should look for ways that your product or service will expand the authority, power base, influence, or resources of someone in the room. In many cases, this is more of a by-product of solving your customer's stated problem—and in most cases, your champion will quickly reveal his unique interest in helping you succeed. You should know that prior to your meetings so that you can keep your eyes and ears open for signs that you have a strong champion prospect.

Early on, pay attention to everyone's response to what you are selling or who you work for. Look for signs that a deal might add some sort of power or success to her life. If you sell the cutting edge, look for the innovators and explorers who gravitate toward radical change like moths to a flame. Don't be intimidated if they initially debate you; it's a sign of their interest in promoting change and out-of-the-box thinking.

When you identify a good candidate, cultivate a personal relationship to serve as the icing on the cake. Be a good listener. Don't be afraid to challenge his point of view, so long as you can back it up. The resulting bond can keep the champion engaged through thick and thin, especially when you might ask her to push for your company quite stringently down the line.

Some words of caution are required here. First of all, you need to know the difference between an account friend and a superfriend who will champion you. Legendary venture capitalist Mark Suster, who started out as an enterprise technology sales executive, learned this lesson the hard way. He warns against finding champions who are actually people with no influence and no authority (or NINAs).

It's easy to gain false confidence when you think you have someone in your corner you believe can do all the heavy lifting. You can even convince yourself that you don't need to do the selling. "This is one of the most common mistakes untrained people make in the sales process," said Mark, "because the nice guy you're talking to tells you not to worry about the others, that he has you covered."[6] In some cases, he'll say that he wants to play the role of the "filter," controlling all the information coming into the company, presumably in order to make him more powerful. In others, the NINA has a false sense of confidence that her pitch ability is good enough to rep your service.

Either way, here's the point: maintain control over the process and think of your champion as an extension of the team and not a replacement for it. Your team has worked too hard to get you to this point for you to let go and risk letting the untrained do your job.

Then there's the misfit or lackey scenario, in which your champion hurts your cause. "Having a low, no-credibility champion is worse than having no champion at all," said Steve Kaplan. "You need to ask yourself, does this person shine a positive light on me and my company?" You can suss this out early on by keeping your eyes open, paying attention to how the group dynamics are playing out. When your champion candidate offers up an idea, how is it received? Do others engage with his observations, or does he receive the brush-off?

You can also measure the champion's cred factor by looking at her level of access to and influence with the key decision makers who will pull the trigger. Sometimes, you'll start out connecting with a lateral champion with credibility, then leverage that relationship to discover and develop other champions further up the ladder. In some high-dollar or high-complexity sales, it will take multiple champions to win.

Once you find the high-credibility, highly motivated champion, make sure you arm her for success, especially if she has to rep you in remote situations where you will never be invited to present. Make sure she's got the most essential data, key slides, and relevant case studies at her fingertips. If you are close enough, you can offer to run through a presentation and role-play with her, with you assuming the role of one of the influencers inside her company. By doing this, you can ensure she's properly prepared to "sell your idea forward." Never assume that she gets it like you do; if you fail to prep her, it could lead to an embarrassing situation on her part, which brings me to the last point.

When I asked John Livesay how he kept Andrea Chao engaged throughout such a long sales cycle, he said, "I constantly made sure that she looked good in front of her boss." He never took her for granted, and he made sure she lost no internal clout by throwing her weight behind his cause. He treated her with mad respect.

You, too, can enable your champion to be best informed by sharing knowledge. Find ways to add value to the deal that she can take credit for. And most of all, never leave her hanging with a loose detail. After all, that's what friends do. Especially with their biz besties.

The Deal Mentor

Mentors appear throughout Greek mythology and are coded into our psyche as those who lead heroes to success in difficult situations. The mentor first appears in literature in Homer's *Odyssey*. Goddess Athena takes on the character of Mentor to help Telemachus on his quest to reunite with his father and save the kingdom after the Trojan War. She gave him encouragement, but most of all she gave him gifts.

In his book *Morphology of the Folktale*, historian Vladimir Propp identifies the function of the mentor as a donor or provider: "one who temporarily aids the hero, usually by giving some gift. It may be a magic weapon, an important key or clue . . . or a life-saving piece of advice."[7] Think about modern culture where mentors like Miyagi (*The Karate Kid*) or Yoda (*Star Wars*) provide the hero exactly what he needs for the next battle.

Sometimes, when you are stuck in the sales game, you need a deal mentor's advice. You might need an unbiased view into what it takes to penetrate a company or succeed in its culture. Unlike the inside champion, the deal mentor only gives advice and is often outside the prospect company or not involved in the buying process. They can be colleagues you've worked with in the past, ex-employees of the prospect company, or associates who have successfully sold to this prospect specifically or in this industry.

Alex Banayan, a venture associate with Alsop Louie Partners, is considered a superconnector in tech circles. Named as one of the most powerful people in finance by *Business Insider,* he's the youngest venture capital firm partner in the history of Silicon Valley.[8] Banayan has invested in and advised several B2B technology startups. He's also been "sold to" by scores of company founders. Deal mentors, in his belief, are very useful in the dealstorming process and throughout the whole life cycle of selling.

"In a lot of cases, finding a deal mentor can be the most important part of the sales process," he told me. "You can do all the right things, and make all the right plans, but the deal can fall apart without the mentor's vision." His point is that often we bat blind and come out swinging at the wrong targets. "Without a deal mentor, it's like you are stumbling through an unlit room, blind to the darkness," he warned. "With one, you have night vision goggles."

When someone gives you insights about who to talk to, what to focus on during the pitch, and which buttons to push, you can dramatically reduce the sales cycle. Each time we do something clumsy, usually because of our ignorance about the prospect situation, we take two steps back. When we know something the competition doesn't know about the sales process, we take leaps forward.

The search for your deal mentor starts with the question "Who knows something about this prospect?" This applies to the decision maker, company, or in some cases, the industry. Much like organizing a dealstorming team, this question helps frame your efforts to find someone who can give you unique insights, not just encouragement.

Deal mentors can come from anywhere in the organization. Startup guru Mark Suster has a name for insiders with the ability and desire to mentor potential suppliers—sages. "Most organizations are filled with 'sages' who have been there a long period of time and know the organization and its systems inside and out," he said. "I used to meet sages by walking the halls and talking to people randomly."[9] You may very well find them during the same initial meetings where you are looking for champions.

While they won't advocate your cause or play informant on competitors, they still add value. "The sage is important in helping you to understand the systems, people, and processes of a company," Mark says. "They know why things are the way they are." In many cases, they enjoy sharing this information, especially if they work in a company they feel is too bureaucratic or secretive.

In some situations, your deal mentor may be a coworker at your company. He is likely to be forthcoming with insights, and if he worked there pretty recently—his information is still fresh. You don't necessarily have to add him to the team if all you need is a simple piece of strategic insight. But remember the Sterling example from Chapter 4, where sales spent considerable time conferring with internal SAP experts when they were amply informed already. Double-check that you really need expert peer advice before you invest precious time to locate, brief, and meet with one.

Ravi Gundlapalli led the supply chain management program for Boeing at E2open, a startup that sells supply chain technology solutions. When one of their sales executives was assigned the Boeing account, he met with Ravi for the inside scoop. "I told him how new programs were funded in that group," Ravi told me. "I also warned him about what blocked potential deals there and how their culture worked when it came to engaging with new suppliers."

This accelerated the sales executive's efforts, helping him to quickly make inroads. Later, when that sales exec was tasked with selling to Raytheon, a competitor to Boeing, Ravi was tapped again as a deal mentor. While he didn't have inside information per se, he knew them well as a competitor and was able to give good advice on pain points and hot buttons.

Your sales challenge may not only be external. In many cases, the challenge comes internally, likely due to silo mentality, which makes it hard to execute company-wide deals. This was the situation Jay Samit faced while working at Sony in the early 2000s. He was tasked with putting together corporate partnerships that integrated brands across the companies' various devices, properties, and networks.

"Sony is arguably the most siloed company in history," he says. "Executing a deal between divisions was nearly impossible due to politics. The reason that the Walkman group couldn't create an iPod killer was due to the lack of an onboard hard drive. That was the Vaio (computer) group's domain, and they couldn't touch it."

When Jay had Coca-Cola on the hook for an eight-million-dollar integrated sponsorship deal, he had to figure out how to sell it to every division of the company, both in the United States and Japan. He built relationships across business units, one meeting at a time, by being ambitious yet humble. "I'd approach the group manager at Sony TV and I'd tell him that I'm new here, and eager to find a way to make a difference. . . . 'You are very important as a leader, and I would appreciate you giving me a roadmap to how your team works,'" he said.

Jay was careful never to lead by trying to sell Coca-Cola, or brand integration of any sorts, and listened much more than he talked. "The more he [the group manager] would teach me, the more invested he became in my success," he said. Jay was good at following up on conversations with notes as well as demonstrations that he was truly learning how they operated. Much like the mentor in mythology enthuses at the student's progress, his mentors took delight in schooling him.

In just a few months, Jay traversed the entire set of Sony's strategic business units, picking up unlikely mentors in high places who were attracted to his self-effacing but ambitious approach.

At some point, deep into the conversations, Jay would introduce the Coke promotional opportunity, mostly using it as an example of how he was trying to navigate the empire successfully to produce win-wins. Even though many group heads initially were resistant to any type of company-wide idea, by that point "they were so in the soup with me, they didn't want our program to fail." Their budding relationship produced the necessary shock absorbers he needed to overcome their objections, ask for favors, and, in the end, close a historic deal for Sony and Coca-Cola.

The best source of deal mentorship is your extended network of friends and colleagues. Find someone who's recently been successful selling a comparable product or service to yours, and you have a strong candidate.

Since he went to work at Oracle, a longtime friend of mine has been bombarded with requests from friends who want to know how to best engage with this high-tech giant. He sold to Oracle when he worked at a startup, and now that he works on the inside, he's developed a sharp outlook on the do's and don'ts of doing business with this company.

"When a friend tells me he's about to pitch Oracle a cloud-based solution, I'll give him some guidance," he told me. "I'll warn him not to pitch bigger ideas below the VP level or that if you're a cloud vendor, you better go through the security review process up front as part of your approach or you'll never get through procurement." While none of this is proprietary information, still, it's solid gold for a deal-storm team.

If you don't know a good deal mentor candidate directly, LinkedIn and other social networks make it easier than ever to identify potential ones. You can use their search functionality to find matches or even post updates, asking for assistance. You can also use your own email groups at work to look for someone who has sold to or works for your target prospect.

Finding someone who knows something about your target is just the beginning, though. You still need to give her a reason to help you. Most often, the reason a mentor decides to help you is because she likes you, she is attracted to your enthusiasm, or what you are trying to accomplish for your company and your prospect resonates with her.

My second book, *The Likeability Factor,* identified that people like you if you make them feel good or have made a difference to them. So be positive when you pitch to a potential mentor. Because most people these days will look at your online profiles after meeting you, be helpful and generous in all your status updates and posts. Be audacious about what you want to accomplish for the prospect and confident about your ability to add to the prospect's success if given the chance.

The best way to woo a mentor is to bring the gift of knowledge to every conversation. Be a voracious reader and thought leader through constant sharing of cutting-edge information and game-changing perspectives. When people perceive you as a giver, they are usually ready to reciprocate by telling you what they know. This has been my go-to strategy throughout my career for finding mentors, whether I'm looking inside the prospect or out into the market.

Beyond spreading good ideas or sharing helpful perspectives, you can also play the role of deal mentor. After all, it's a puzzle out there for everyone, including your next potential partner. This was the perspective of Tom Kane, CEO of wireless cell site developer NB+C. For years, his company had specialized in site location, construction, and maintenance of cell sites. Tom is always on the lookout for expansion opportunities, especially into new and lucrative services.

"When LTE 4G [technology] came to market, it became apparent that not only would the cell site architecture need to be modified, carriers would also need a fiber upgrade," he told me. "This is a little outside our normal scope of work, but one of my top guys convinced me we could figure it out quickly and be good at it." While they had confidence, absent a track record in that space, they'd need to gain the prospect's trust.

When his team learned that Comcast was going after the master contract for providing fiber to T-Mobile, Tom saw a dual opportunity: help Comcast succeed with T-Mobile and convince them to bring NB+C in on the contract. He had dozens of people at the company with experience working with T-Mobile on multiple fronts, from procurement to quality to corporate planning.

Tom made the rounds with his team, gathering facts and stories about what does and doesn't work with T-Mobile, how they approach site development and who their current set of technology and bandwidth providers are as well as the company's strengths and weaknesses. Armed with a treasure trove of insights, he and his team talked to their Comcast connections and agreed to mentor them on the pitch to T-Mobile.

"Our intel was the core of Comcast's presentation to T-Mobile," says Tom. "I was there as their partner. It was the key to their win." The resulting fiber services contract for Comcast called for a variety of services the company did not provide, including real estate due diligence. The Comcasters on the deal team returned Tom's mentorship by providing NB+C insights on how to win this business, from real estate due diligence services to the plum work of modifying cell sites for LTE 4G.

Soon, Tom's work paid off with a fat new revenue stream with a new strategic partner, Comcast. Tom's team won business in their core as well as for the new division they created to modify cell sites for new wireless technologies and the infrastructure that goes along with them. The trust they'd garnered with key Comcast contacts during their moment of need gave them time to climb the learning curve on an entirely new set of services.

In a world of people who are always asking to "show them the love," he found a way for his company to stand out by being the uncon-ditional giver. His triumph echoes the philosophy of Paul McCartney when he wrote, "the love you take is equal to the love you make."

CHAPTER 10

Innovation at the Relationship Exchange

For sales leaders, it's critical to nurture an innovative culture so your team can tackle an increasingly complex market. Your account executives, as problem owners, must employ creative thinking, make unexpected connections, or champion a novel idea. While the process I've outlined in this book gives them an engine for problem solving via dealstorming, the process requires fuel: motivation, resources, resilience, and competence. And this fuel comes from you.

In the context of business-to-business sales, creativity is truly nurture over nature.

Real solutions are created as people make powerful connections with each other. Your job is to foster those relationships inside your group, and, whenever possible, throughout the enterprise.

When I asked CareerBuilder's Eric Gilpin to give me an example of a truly innovative salesperson, he quickly nominated Alyssa DeMattos, sharing the story about how she led her team against great odds to the company's greatest victory. He hired her out of a bad situation a decade ago, when she was working for a model recruiting agency that was, in her words, "soul sucking."

Though Alyssa didn't have any business-to-business sales experience, Eric saw tremendous potential in her, so he gave her a chance. She responded to the opportunity by applying herself, working long hours to develop her knowledge and skill set. Within a few years, she rose from inside sales rep to field account executive with President's Club performance.

In 2011, after demonstrating her professional growth and loyalty to his professional goals, Eric rewarded her with the Allegis opportunity. "They were very upset with us, and I knew that it would take someone special to bring them back," he said. "I took inventory of my entire sales team to find the right person for the job. Alyssa demonstrated a unique way of getting people to lower the wall and at the same time take care of CareerBuilder. That was the winning combo for me."

Besides handing her a huge account opportunity, he extended something even more important: his trust. "I gave her all the rope she needed for this one," he told me. "Many of the things she wanted to do seemed cheesy or, at the very least, risky to me. She said she knew what she was doing, and I believed her. In the end, her ability to always get it right with the customers taught me a lot about myself as a leader and how I have to challenge my own assumptions."

Alyssa's success didn't stem merely from her creativity. The innovations she and her team pulled off were enabled by powerful leader-member relationships. She had air cover to pursue the new, and a burning desire to bring it home for the company. This theme showed up in every successful dealstorm I've been involved in.

At Yahoo!, the ValueLab team's success was made possible because of my relationships with our sales leader, Anil Singh, and then later his replacement, Greg Coleman. They trusted me, supported me, and rewarded my team and me for our account wins. And we worked our butts off for them. It wasn't just about the company. We wanted to make them look good for backing us.

John Livesay succeeded in his comeback at *W* due in large part to his relationship with Nina Lawrence, vice president and publisher, and Susan Keena, associate publisher. They both admired him for his skills and know-how. When he made the big ask, requesting editorial involvement on a sales issue, they did it. He didn't let them down, either. "When you work for people who believe in you," he told me, "you believe in yourself even more."

In my interviews for this book, I noted these relationships but didn't make the connection to how fundamental they were to innovation in the sales process until I stumbled upon an academic paper on creativity in the sales process by Ieva Martinaityte and Claudia Sacramento at Aston Business School in the United Kingdom.[1]

"Most research so far has focused on informing [sales] managers about how they can help their followers to become more creative," they write. "However, this might not be sufficient to lead them to higher job performance levels." After conducting a tightly controlled study, they concluded, "To the extent that employee creativity is related to sales depends on the quality of the leader-member exchange (LMX)."

The LMX concept, in a nutshell, is expressed by a leader offering a salesperson opportunity, support, and latitude. In return, the salesperson offers creativity, commitment, and loyalty to the leader's goals and needs. As they increase in their offers to each other, these exchanges add up to a high leader-member relationship. This in turn creates mutual trust and respect, which converts creativity into innovation, which is best defined as "when solutions successfully find their way to market."[2]

When the exchange level between the sales leader and salesperson is low, the leader withholds opportunities to work on complex sales or coaching on how a salesperson is doing in a difficult situation. The leader doesn't trust the salesperson, so anything off the script or out of the system is summarily rejected.

In many cases, the research suggests that when the salesperson doesn't feel trusted, she loses her motivation or lacks the confidence to suggest or champion the new. Or worse, if she isn't getting feedback on how her ideas are playing out, she doesn't learn the difference between a new approach and an effective one and makes errors in the field, making the relationship even weaker.

As I mentioned earlier, creativity is one's ability to produce novel work that is appropriate to the situation. This requires a combination of confidence, commitment, and competency. The quality of your relationships, then, determines the extent of your team member's ability to successfully solve sales challenges that are beyond your current sales process. And it doesn't stop there. The leader-member exchange determines how innovative each person in a dealstorm will be—which will determine its success.

The True Nature of Relationships

Relationships are like wireless phone connections. When they are strong, they produce a clear and satisfying conversation. When they are weak, they produce frustration and are unproductive. The key, then, is to boost the strength of the connection. While your phone call depends on a strong network and functional equipment, leader-member relationships rely on a sound perspective and effective practices.

First things first: leaders don't have relationships with their teams. They have relationships with individuals. LMX researchers point this out often, explaining that relationships are always dyads and connections between two people only. I can't tell you how many times I've heard someone say, "I have a [great/bad] relationship with this group," or "I'm trying to develop trust with my team." This perspective is flawed. It leads to sweeping generalizations that ignore the uniqueness of each human being and her need to be recognized as a person and not a cog in the machine.

You need to invest time to develop your relationship with each individual that you bring on your sales team or into your dealstorm. I know—that's more work than focusing on just the rock stars or lumping them together. But it's the only way you can truly connect with the essence of the other, which is the foundation of the leader-member exchange.

Next, understand that relationships are based on exchanges, not intentions. You cannot will yourself to have a good relationship with one of your team members. Conversely, people cannot force a relationship on you, due to their desire to fit in or succeed. Relationships are built not with thoughts or needs. They are developed through thoughtful deeds.

Emotional connections are fueled by the give and give between you and the other. Give and take may work in a negotiation, but mutual generosity is the key to relationships. Regardless of how much you found in common early or how attractive his track record or background looked, the relationship grows from what you give each other over time.

It starts with the first offer, which is the leader's duty. The offer can start with advice—on how to be successful, fit in, and handle problems. The member may respond with a reciprocal offer of applying that knowledge in practice. Now, the ball is back in the leader's court; she needs to notice the member's effort and then make the next offer. And so on. As these offers add up over time, the strength of the connection grows. The key idea here is that an offer has value in the eyes of the recipient, triggering a feeling, which in this case is obligation. This is not a bad concept, either, because the exchange must be constantly energized so as to keep going.

Leaders need to size up what their members actually need in order to succeed, reduce stress, or find work satisfaction. In my experience, the best leaders use design thinking in order to find the best offers they can make to their members. They look at where the member is in his career path and either widen it for him or suggest a new route. Like any designer, the leader takes into account the emotional experience as much as the practical implications.

In *Group Genius*, author Keith Sawyer uses improv comedy as an analogy for effective innovation at work. In improv, one player makes an offer, which is then accepted by another player, then countered with an acceptable offer. Eventually, a novel performance occurs, usually to the delight of the audience. The improv process breaks down, though, when someone cuts off the joke by missing or refusing the offer.

For leaders, it's critical to keep your eyes and ears open for offers by your team members. The offer could be an effort to learn or a willingness to work on improving skills or hustle factor. Each time you detect an offer, it's critical you respond with something of equal or greater value so that the story continues to build upon itself.

While I've focused on work currency so far in these exchanges, it's important to point out that your members also value your respect, liking, and acknowledgment. While these might be ephemeral compared with offering big opportunities or coaching, they still contribute to a stronger connection.

Don't give up on relationships if your offers to members aren't always reciprocated. As a leader, you need to be self-aware enough to rise above the occasional broken link in the relationship chain and either try again or point out to your member that you are making an effort toward developing the relationship. A leader, by definition, should lead the relationship. Researchers find that just talking about the effort can kick-start a healthy set of exchanges, leading to high LMX.

Rewarding Exchanges That Drive Innovation

Not every offer of value drives performance. The leader-member exchange functions like a swap meet, where the most successful traders have a keen sense of the true value of an offer. Some swap meet items are treasures and others are just junk. Knowing the difference is the key to fair trades that profit both sides of the table.

In the case of the leader-member swap meet, it's a matter of finding offers that are valued and also drive business performance. In her landmark study, published in the *Journal of Personal Selling and Sales Management*, Professor Susan DelVecchio lays out the right stuff: "The manager allows more latitude to salespeople who are seen as more competent and loyal. These exchanges and the quality of the salesperson-manager relationship may be especially important when the sales task requires adaptive selling behaviors."[3]

Salespeople appreciate receiving freedom to chart their own course, solve problems on their own, and forge relationships as they see fit. It's in the DNA of the selling persona to equate latitude with being respected as a top producer. The most talented players value autonomy above all. In DelVecchio's study, this was verified in B2B sales: "Not all contributions [by managers] are equally important. Salespeople in this sample evaluate the relationship with his or her manager as of higher quality when he or she is the recipient of managerial latitude." Other offers like encouragement, financial rewards, or social opportunities paled in comparison.

During the organizational phase, sponsors should reward a problem owner's competency and loyalty with latitude. If you trust him, then give him a lot of freedom to pick his team, write his deal brief and run his meeting. If you really trust him, you may give him free rein to launch dealstorm projects or implement solutions with instructions to "ask you for approval when he thinks it's required."

And to flip this around—if your salesperson isn't experienced, or you haven't built up trust yet, you need to tightly manage the process as a sponsor. I know that this takes more time on your part, but the dealstorm resource qualifying formula from Chapter 4 takes care of that. It's a big opportunity by definition. You'll need to review the team he's putting together, go over his deal brief, and actively participate in meetings and implementation steps.

In all of the research I've reviewed, our trust of salespeople comes down to his or her competence and loyalty. Competence is a combination of product, prospect and process knowledge, and core skills, such as communication, financial, technical and interpersonal. That's why it's important for leaders to turn up their noticing knob to observe more than just the sales figures.

Don't solely rely on numbers. Trust people based on a combination of measurable and intangible attributes. Give extra credit for those who display a commitment to getting better at their craft and gaining a deeper understanding of how the business works.

Professional loyalty is defined as "the expression of public support for the goals and personal character of the manager."[4] I think of it as the salesperson's alignment with the vision, goals, and professional needs of her manager. (I'm assuming here that the manager has the company's interests in mind, too.)

When you perceive that someone is highly competent, shares your goals, and respects you, you develop trust that she'll do you right. You know that she won't let you down, in part due to her ability and in part as a result of her commitment to you. For some, the ability to trust can be a challenge. But if you want to build effective leader-member relationships, you must extend latitude. You will only receive back what you are willing to extend.

In the above-mentioned Aston Business School study, it is recommended that the manager support the salesperson as she attempts to creatively solve a sales problem. Skillsoft's Danielle Saurer received support from her manager via pricing analyst resources as she internally sold the idea of folding Skillsoft's training into their partner's HR platform. "This gave me even more motivation to make it work," she told me.

The researchers also pointed out another vital form of support, the willingness to back a salesperson when faced with adversity. Early in his tenure at Sony, Jay Samit spun up a cobranding deal with McDonald's, worth millions of dollars and precious distribution for Sony's nascent digital music program. When he pitched it to Sony's board of directors in Tokyo, board members initially rejected it because "they didn't want their logo on a greasy burger box."

During the meeting, newly appointed CEO Howard Stringer fought for Jay's idea, standing up and asking them all, "If we aren't doing programs like this, then why am I here?!" He stared down his directors in a tense moment, which led to them approving the deal. "From that point on," Jay said, "I gave everything I had not only to continue to find new opportunities for Sony, but to make Howard look good for going to bat for me."

So here's the formula for high-LMX relationships that work: leaders extend latitude and support in exchange for competence and loyalty. Your team members value autonomy and resources, so in the swap meet of corporate work, you'll see them respond to the offer almost every time.

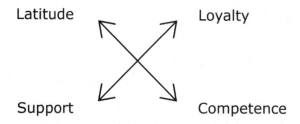

As long as you match their efforts to improve and abide, they will continue to double down on improving their competency. As you extend trust and unflagging support, you'll gain their intense loyalty. It's a virtuous cycle of leader-member relationship development that can only lead to spectacular alliances and breakthrough work.

Widening the Circle

While you realistically can't develop high-LMX relationships with every one of your salespeople, you can widen your inner circle by coaching competence and inspiring loyalty. This allows you to improve your relationships with more team members for the right reason, lifting their ability to solve sales challenges. In other words, this will help you scale innovative selling throughout your group.

There's a side benefit you'll see from your efforts as well. In DelVecchio's study, high-value exchanges between leaders and their members improved the rep's ability to execute adaptive selling, which is foundational to sales methodologies such as the Challenger Sale, Miller Heiman Strategic Selling, SPIN Selling, Solution Selling, or Diagnostic Business Development.

The first step in coaching competency is to show everyone the way to continual improvement. You should coach competency in everyone, not just your low-LMX members. We live in times of change, from markets to demographics to technology. Today's smart and superskilled producers can become tomorrow's newest member of the out crowd if they don't keep sharpening the saw.

At the beginning of standing meetings, always offer resources for gaining knowledge or skills. It could be a relevant book, a piece of research, or an upcoming seminar. This hammers home your commitment to growing your team members' competency. When you have your periodic check-in (which should occur at least every quarter), punctuate your account and performance review with suggested courses, books, or exercises.

When I worked for Stan Woodward at Broadcast.com, he advised me to "go shopping in the learning management system" as I prepped for my annual review with my reports. This was a practice at Ascend, the tech company he came from. Too often, we go to the annual review with a rating (e.g., "meets expectations") and some statement about the bonus or compensation. Add specific learning recommendations to each review, and you'll move your team members to a more positive place.

During all of these discussions and meetings, dangle job autonomy or project latitude as the carrot they can have if they improve their knowledge and skills. The DelVecchio study found that managers should be explicit about the freedom to operate that they are giving their salespeople during the performance appraisal, and being clear about how they can extend it. For most salespeople, having more rope is the greatest motivation to bone up on their studies, ask more questions about the market or the product, and improve.[5]

One of the best ways to coach competency is to promote and reward peer mentorship. Your "in-crowd" members can be your best motivators and teachers. Explain that you are evaluating their leadership capabilities and want them to "make everyone around them better." Pair an in-crowd member with a struggling salesperson, and have them work on a specific sales challenge together. Or have him join a dealstorm as a cosponsor.

Final thought on coaching: if the above doesn't work, sit down with your out-crowd member and be candid about his situation. I'm not talking about a warning or performance improvement process (PIP), either. I mean sit down, look him in the eye, and tell him that you want to have a better working relationship with him but that you can only have those with members who are up to speed and getting better every day. Help him understand that's the only way you can be an effective manager.

Your extra effort and focus on building a professional relationship can produce remarkable results. Studies suggest that your low-LMX members are just waiting for you to make the right move for the right reasons. Whatever you offer in exchange for a better relationship will usually produce a response,[6] which makes everything else work so much better. People want to form relationships; it's in our nature.

You will best inspire ongoing loyalty by being transparent about your business goals and vision for the group. Constantly reinforce what you see as best-practices and win-win business dealings in every conversation, meeting, or account review. Take the time to create a document—your manifesto—and circulate it to everyone on your team, updating it as times change or your leadership's focus shifts.

Loyalty to your professional needs and character ensures that members know when to draw the line, ask permission, or just say no. It produces a strong sense of obligation that they don't let you down. It's personal. That's why it's something you should reward in a relationship.

Many sales leaders I've interviewed echo the vision of their CEO or leadership team, and then provide more information on how the business really works. They often have discussions after a key release, earnings announcement, or speech so everyone on the team understands what's going on and why certain decisions were made. In this case, you are showing your loyalty to your top leader and the company. This inspires your charges to weigh corporate interests as they contemplate innovations.

Given that you desire loyalty to your charter for the enterprise, it's important that you focus on the purpose of the company. At Abbott Labs, leaders reinforce the value of the medicines they are bringing to market to save lives and how every sales rep can make a difference by doing their job well and abiding by all regulations. Leaders at Prudential Retirement Services stress how they are humanizing retirement for employees at companies and making sure families have enough set aside for the future. Where there is purpose, there is passion.

One of my mentors, Stanley Marcus Jr., told me about how he inspired loyalty in his associates. He shared with them that Neiman

Marcus employed thousands of people, creating a livelihood for their families. The company created wealth for their suppliers as well as the communities where they operated. "But the company is just like a baby," he would explain. "It needs to be looked after carefully by all of us in order to survive." In his experience, transferring responsibility to associates motivated them to "dot their i's and cross their t's every time."

As you widen the in crowd, you are deepening your relationships with more members, expanding the level of sales innovation throughout your group. You will inspire more members to approach sales challenges creatively and courageously.

While all this coaching and inspiring sounds like a lot of extra work, the latitude you'll be able to extend will save you time. You won't have to constantly look over everyone's shoulder or micromanage accounts or dealstorms as much. But this only works if you are willing to trust people who have demonstrated their competence and loyalty.

For those of you with trust issues (you know who you are), test and scale the freedom you give your in crowd, and objectively measure how often they do you right. If you pay attention closely, you'll find that in a high-LMX relationship, you really can let go.

Strengthening the 'Storm

Project leaders can drive innovation by forging strong relationships with each member of the team. Researchers at the University of Colorado and the University of Louisville studied the correlation between LMX quality and innovative problem-solving behavior in industrial R&D work groups and found that the two were highly related. When the bonds between the leader and member are strong, it creates a rich climate for pattern recognition and creativity, leading to rapid problem solving.[7]

To lead the perfect dealstorm, you must create high-quality relationships with your team members. This requires you to make high-value offers to them that trigger reciprocation. Through my experience, I've learned that in this situation, the leader should offer respect and recognition in exchange for each member's engagement and collaboration. It's the currency of working groups, especially when participation is voluntary. As they swap those offers, their bonds grow tighter.

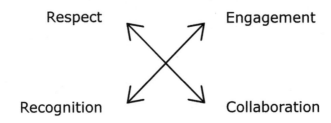

Respect   Engagement

Recognition   Collaboration

Because the dealstorm project requires us to work interdependently, it's important for the problem owner to establish high LMX with as many team members as possible. This means it's an ongoing task, where some connections will happen right away and others will be a work in progress right up until the end.

Your first offer is respect. When people agree to join your sales challenge project, they are taking on work that's usually outside of their job description. From reading the deal brief thoroughly to participating in meetings and resulting project work, they must invest quite a bit of time. So respect their time at every step of the way.

That's why the deal brief should be effective yet concise. Your meetings need to be long enough to create results, but as compact as possible. Meetings need to feel short, even when they go for more than an hour. This is a matter of facilitating them to keep a brisk pace and avoid distractions. They must start and stop on time. Reporting after a meeting confirms that you value everyone's time and that the meeting wasn't just a conversation.

Next, you need to respect each member's intelligence. This is one of our greatest professional needs. Never talk down to junior members in the group. Talk up a team member's expertise when you introduce him, focusing on how it can be leveraged during the meeting.

When a resource offers up a potential solution, the facilitator must enforce the "ideas can come from anywhere" rule in the event that an insider reacts dismissively because of its source. When a subject matter expert offers an opinion without any specific data or case studies, accept it on its face in the moment while reminding yourself that it's subject to postmeeting verification. Recognize that people can get up to speed on your sales challenge pretty quickly, and that intelligence is not static. During a good dealstorm, resources get a lot smarter about the situation at hand.

Finally, respect each member's feelings. Like it or not, there will be suggestions or plans that trigger an emotional response. A resource may fear increased workload or exposure to senior-level executives. Someone may get frustrated at a lack of progress. A member may get angry with another participant due to an insensitive remark. That's the risk of bringing together a diverse group.

Your job is not to fix those feelings with a "you shouldn't feel that way." That only pushes people away. Your job is to let team members share those feelings. In *The 8th Habit*, Dr. Stephen Covey revealed that most people exhibiting negative emotions don't want you to do anything other than let them be heard. From arbitration to personal relationships, he's found that treating "feelings as facts" often releases the injured party from the pain and lets him or her move on.

As you offer these forms of respect, you'll usually be rewarded with engagement. Create a respectful environment, and you'll usually garner attention and command energy. As your dealstorm participants demonstrate willingness to learn, contribute to the discussion, and participate in the building of deliverables, you must counter with recognition.

At Yahoo!, I often sent thank-you cards to resources. Alyssa DeMattos sent cookies to engineers with handwritten notes. When you show appreciation like that, it goes a long way toward creating a one-to-one connection. But be careful; sharing private recognition with noncontributors will come off as insincere because people know when they did or did not make a difference in a situation. Public recognition, on the other hand, delivers a social currency. During his postmeeting reports, John Livesay itemized his appreciation for specific contributions that individuals or small groups made to the Guess project.

And while words can work, nothing shows the love like action. The eight CareerBuilder engineers who built the Allegis prototype were given the Spirit of Excellence Award at the 2012 sales kickoff meeting. Mark Schmitz at SAP Cloud invites someone outside of his group—a lead from finance or legal who has made countless contributions to deal-solving projects—to the President's Club sales incentive trip each year. "It's a little thing we do that can really unify an organization," he said.

One caveat: recognize specific deeds, not ideas. Itemize what he or his small group found, created, researched, or built. Be very specific. You can also recognize the time that someone invested, because effort should be appreciated. Remember that good ideas come from a series of improvements, in most cases involving so many resources that the lines of ownership are blurred.

When I played in a rock band and our jam session produced a new tune, it was everybody's, even if I brought the lyric or our guitarist offered the first riff. It took all of us to make it tuneful. Sharing the creative credit led to harmony, and so it will be when you share the glory of problem-solving credit as well.

So long as your team member reciprocates your offers of value, you will develop a high-LMX relationship. But in some cases, you'll need to inspire engagement or coach collaboration—the two currencies you seek as the problem owner. The onus is on you to keep it going.

Respect drives engagement, especially in the beginning. Never assume that someone will maintain the same energy level or openness throughout a long deal cycle. Don't let the exchange become one-sided or you'll eventually disconnect with him.

If you follow the process outlined in Chapter 6, you'll facilitate engagement by keeping things interesting, moving toward action, and enabling people to participate by taming the conversation hogs. Keep your eyes open for someone who wants to speak up but can't find an insert point or is too timid. Use the templates for problem or solution finding to provide a framework for discussion, which is important to keeping everyone in the discussion.

Group dynamics require justice; so don't let a noncontributor slide. Either talk to him privately at the break about it, or call on him to share an idea or opinion. If all else fails, don't invite him to future meetings, or tell him that it's not working out and that the team should move on without him. It will send a powerful signal to the rest of the group that participation—not just attendance—is required.

Coaching collaboration between people who don't work together normally or share different priorities will be your hardest leadership challenge. Since it involves sharing information and building upon the work of others, you'll need to practice what you preach. During meetings at Yahoo!, I often revealed "something you might not know about the sales world" to the group, such as "All of our goals and projections are essentially guesses," which often resulted in a show-and-tell exchange in which an engineer might respond, "Most of our coding is done in the middle of the night!" It's a good icebreaker that breaks down walls and inspires empathy. During the meetings, keep asking the group, "What else do we not know that could make a difference?" The more you dig, the more your resources will likely offer.

Cross-pollinate personalities to work together on improving or executing ideas. Keep your ears open for common backgrounds or personal affinities that can deformalize the situation and lead to a willingness to partner up. When someone launches a critique of an idea, ask him how he might improve it, and when he does, what the new benefit of the idea might be. Celebrate new alliances and friendships.

You'll bring out teamwork best by making sure that the goal of your dealstorm transcends the departmental needs of each of your members. That's why I love to focus on beating the competition and achieving excellence or the pursuit of finding the truth. Focusing only on the revenue isn't enough to get others to let down their guard, reveal what they know, and work with corporate strangers.

As with sales leaders, the problem owner must keep the exchange going with everyone in the dealstorm. Never take relationships you've forged for granted. There is no end to the amount of sincere respect and recognition you can offer. At each milestone of your dealstorm, take some time to reflect on the individual contributions your resources and sponsor are making. Think about how important they are, not just to the enterprise, but also to your personal success. The more time you spend recollecting their efforts, the easier it is to bring the love to the next meeting or exchange.

That's the relationship-building power of gratitude.

Building a Network

So far, I've focused on the value of dealstorming from a solutions standpoint: getting deals done and sales challenges solved. But there's a side benefit to the process with a potent upside. You just may build a network of relationships throughout your company that fosters a culture of creative collaboration that propels it forward through all kinds of challenges.

Even though the connections you'll build will start out professional in nature, eventually they get personal. As you grow in your appreciation of others, you'll find common ground, and a surprising result will follow. You'll like the account executive a lot as a person. You'll cherish as a friend the engineer you sat next to in a dealstorm.

You may be asked to help on a finance group presentation or to participate in a project planning session that requires input from a field-level salesperson. Participate fully. Bring the same energy and effort to others' projects that you expected them to bring to your dealstorm. Keep the fire burning.

We complain a lot about how silo mentality keeps companies from being productive, innovative, or agile. In reality, it's hard to break them down. As long as we organize into managed groups with limited resources, protectiveness will harden them against outside forces. Your company likely deals with this, and so do your competitors.

By forging cross-departmental connections around big challenges, you can lead others to build underground networks of tunnels between the silos. Each one is dug by hand, one dealstorm or collaborative work project at a time. The relationships reinforce each tunnel, brick by brick, so that they can bear the weight of politics and the pressures of the market. They provide a way for resources to move freely across an enterprise.

This redefines what it means to be a sales-driven company. No longer will your group simply produce the revenue that drives the work and keeps the lights on. These relationships can drive the company's ability to innovate through collaboration. There are huge challenges on the horizon for your company in trying to develop new products, break into new markets, improve profit margins, acquire talent, and keep up with the pace of global change. Solving them will be a team sport.

If not you, then who leads this charge? If not now, when do you start digging?

Conclusion: Why Everyone Should Weather a 'Storm

Recently, I reconnected with Stan Woodward, who ignited my dealstorming tendency back in 1997 with his admonishment to "not go down alone." We talked about the good old days for a while before our conversation shifted to the value of teaming up to overcome sales challenges.

"I think everyone should be on a deal team at some point," he said. "I'm not just talking about just sales either—I mean everyone. It teaches the value of teamwork like no other project can." His point was that because there is a final score—deal won/lost, account saved/lost—a deal team sees measurable outcomes from their work. The process that's used to get to the finish line drives home the fact that there is no lone solution maker on the playing field of work. "That's why ex-military are such good hires," he continued. "They clearly understand the value of working together as a team."

Dealstorming not only delivers sales results and improved delivery later, it's a learning platform for every person who participates in the process. For the sales leader, the qualification process adds more sophistication to her pipeline or account review process. Previously, the focus was on revenue projections, status, and how long the opportunity or relationship has been in play. Dealstorming requires the leader to think about the strategic value of the opportunity as well as the degree of difficulty in winning. This prepares her for higher roles in the organization, where these insights are key in allocating resources and prioritizing projects.

Sponsoring a dealstorm requires managing the account executive in a different way: coaching his facilitation technique and problem-solving skills and figuring out how to work across departmental lines. When there is conflict in meetings involving higher-ranking managers, the sponsor must intervene on behalf of the problem owner, which leads to a better understanding of how to manage dysfunction with grace.

For account executives serving as the problem owner, the deal-storming process offers valuable leadership training. They will learn how to recruit resources, including the ability to evaluate skills as well as how to convince others to join the project team and stay engaged over a protracted period of time. Facilitating meetings will provide experience at moving a diverse group through an agenda and keeping them focused on the task at hand. Account executives will be required to ground all assumptions in facts yet inspire their groups to think into the future with an expectation of winning. This is the balance that any manager needs to strike to maintain the respect of his team as well as the energy level to work through challenging situations. As Napoleon Bonaparte said, "The leader's role is to define reality and then give hope."[1]

For all the participants in a dealstorm, the exercise teaches enterprise intelligence at a granular level. No longer will the results from a particular tactic be confined to the black box of the other groups (finance, operations, technology). Through in-meeting discussion and follow-up reports, cause and effect will be clear to everyone involved. Sales group members will better understand the implications of the work they are selling, be it customization, technology integration, or advanced services. Nonsales participants will have a view into the revenue outcomes related to their work. All parties will better understand the politics of the organization, especially when there is disagreement about resource allocation or project prioritization.

Dealstorming truly cuts across the lines, enabling everyone involved to grow.

Sales leaders should make it a goal to ensure that everyone in their groups participates in a dealstorm every year. Even if an account executive doesn't have an opportunity that qualifies for a midsize to large dealstorm, he should participate in one that does, as a resource, information master, or even assistant to the problem owner, doing post-meeting research or entering relevant information into sales force automation. Sales support staff routinely should be injected into dealstorms as resources. It's important, though, that each one have something to offer or have a stake in the outcome. Sales trainers should occasionally audit dealstorms (that is, participate as an observer only) to identify future areas of programming, especially as it relates to project management, communications skills, financial acumen, and technical knowledge.

During meetings involving other department heads, sales leaders should promote dealstorm projects, inviting company-wide collaboration. A powerful question to ask is, "We have an important challenge to resolve. Who wants a voice in this process?" Remember how the sales group at SAP Cloud invites a nonsalesperson to its swanky President's Club incentive meeting each year as a reward for collaborative service? That's a good way to drive home the idea that "ideas can come from anywhere."

Involving your key business partners in a dealstorm can also be a win-win. They might be a reseller, original equipment manufacturer, equipment installer, or systems integrator. Their participation, where it makes sense, helps them to better understand how your business works on multiple levels. They will learn more about dealing with the group dynamics of a diverse team, which will improve their ability to better predict the outcome of their strategies with partners . . . like you.

Earlier I mentioned that in many cases you'll see dealstorm teams form around a sales challenge and gel into an effective group. Likely, they will come together again for new challenges, getting through levels faster as they learn how to work together in applying templates, exercises, or personas against sticking points. That said, it's easy to create dealstorming cliques, which isn't always a good thing.

This was the surprising conclusion that professors Brian Uzzi (Northwestern University) and Jarrett Spiro (Stanford University) came to after analyzing over four hundred Broadway theatrical productions.[2] They created a database of plays, categorizing them by financial success and longevity. They were looking at the correlation between the familiarity of production team members and the outcome of each project. They created a metric (the Q score) to measure the collective working experience that the actors, producers, and writers shared.

Not surprisingly, high Q score teams had a higher success rate than low Q score teams. But there was also a point where too much familiarity produced failure. Above the 3.2 score on the 1 to 5 scale, productions tended to be stale, lack creativity, and ultimately not please critics or early patrons. Because these groups worked together so often, their thinking became more uniform, which prevented them from innovating when out-of-the-box solutions were required. Professors Uzzi and Spiro found that the best teams found the right mix between project veterans and newbies to the process.

So spread around the opportunity, making sure that although certain people learn to work together across groups, you are still injecting new blood into each dealstorm. This is where process and structure meet creativity and innovation. Everyone deserves a chance to learn from and grow through this experience, and according to decades of Broadway play experience, spreading around the opportunity is also good for the bottom line.

With the dealstorming process, you now have a tool that not only produces measureable results, but by its collaborative nature creates influence, power, and transparency for those who lead or participate in one. These side benefits will change your professional life for the better as well as strengthen the fabric of your enterprise over time.

In the case of Alyssa DeMattos, her dealstorming success with Allegis changed her life as much as it has CareerBuilder's business model. Previously, like her sales associates, she had little or no access to other departments at the company. Today, she can pick up the phone and talk to key leads in technology, finance, marketing, or operations—and get results.

"The Allegis team project has brightened the horizons of everyone inside and outside of sales," she said. "Previously, sales naturally took credit for the revenue production, but now everyone in our technology and product groups know that without them, we have nothing to sell." Across CareerBuilder, dealstorms are forming, inspired by Alyssa's success and a growing feeling that as a team, there's nothing the company can't accomplish.

Over the last few years, she's been offered numerous director-level promotions. But she loves the role of account executive, focusing her efforts on wowing her customers, so she's staying put. Even without a lofty management position, she has influence and authority, allowing her to move freely across the company. She gets to have her power and enjoy it, too.

"I'm a leader without a title, working at a company without silos," she exclaimed. In a world where corporate bureaucracy bogs down the best companies, this result is as good as it gets.

And this is the opportunity you have, so peer into your pipeline, find the right opportunity, and spin up a dealstorm today!

I want to hear from you and learn about how you've put this book into practice.

You can help me continue to develop this process with your case studies.

Please contact me: email@timsanders.com.

Acknowledgments

There are so many people who have made a contribution to this book. I'm so grateful to have so much support! I'd like to give heartfelt thanks to:

Shannon Marven, Jan Miller, and Nicki Miser at my literary agency, Dupree Miller. You believed in this project from day one and guided me through the process with love.

My publisher, Portfolio: Natalie Horbachevsky, for being a thoughtful and tenacious editor. You've pushed this manuscript to be clear, effective, and colorful.

Adrian Zackheim, Will Weisser, Hannah Kinisky, Taylor Fleming, and Tara Gilbride—your encouragement and insights have made all the difference. I'm so proud to be one of your authors.

Anthony Cuccia, for producing stellar designs to illustrate concepts inside this book. You helped the abstract get real.

Stan Woodward, for motivating me to create the dealstorming process. You taught me how teamwork makes the impossible merely difficult.

Chris Brogan, for inspiring me to write a book for sales leaders. You thought you were just taking me to dinner, but you changed my life.

To everyone who provided me stories, anecdotes, and case studies for the book. Your insights greatly improved the dealstorming process and will help the readers apply it to their sales challenges.

The sales executives at Broadcast.com, Yahoo!, and my consulting clients for bringing me into the process, closing the deals, and pleasing your customers. None of dealstorming's historical success happens without you!

Notes

Chapter 1: It's Getting Tougher Out There

1. G. Murray et al., "The 2012 IT Buyer Experience Survey: Accelerating the New Buyer's Journey," IDC publication #237207 1:8.
2. Jeffrey Thull, *Mastering the Complex Sale: How to Compete and Win When the Stakes Are High*, 2nd ed. (Hoboken, NJ: Wiley, 2010).
3. Matthew Dixon and Brent Adamson, *The Challenger Sale: Taking Control of the Customer Conversation* (New York: Portfolio, 2011).
4. Both quotes from Dixon and Adamson, *The Challenger Sale: Taking Control of the Customer Conversation*.
5. From "2014 Sales Leadership Forum," announcement by CEB, accessed November 10, 2014, https://www.salesleadershiproundtable.com/SalesForum/events/events .aspx. Based on whitepaper by CEB Marketing Leadership Council in partnership with Google, "The Digital Evolution in B2B Marketing, 2012," last modified May 5, 2015, http://www.executiveboard.com/exbd-resources/content/digital-evolution/ pdf/CEB-Mktg-B2B-Digital-Evolution.pdf.
6. Niamh Whelan-Reiter, "Global Research Shows Mobile and Social Technologies Complicate B2B Sales Processes," last modified November 19, 2013, http:// www.avanade.com/en-us/press-releases/global-research-shows-mobile-and-social -technologies-complicate-b2b-sales-processes-page.
7. Thull, *Mastering the Complex Sale*.
8. Danielle Robinson, "Spin-Offs Add to High-Grade Woes," last modified October 10, 2014, http://www.reuters.com/article/2014/10/10/divestiture-bonds -idUSL2N0S52IR20141010.
9. Tyler Wilde, "A Brief History of Cheats," last modified June 23, 2012, http://www .gamesradar.com/a-brief-history-of-cheats/.

Chapter 2: A Thousand Problems Solved

1. Robert Weisberg, *Creativity: Beyond the Myth of Genius,* 2nd ed. (New York: W. H. Freeman and Co., 1993).

Chapter 3: Sales Genius Is a Team Sport

1. Keith Sawyer, *Group Genius: The Creative Power of Collaboration*, 2nd ed. (New York: Basic Books, 2008).
2. Ibid.
3. Jessica Williams, "Breaking Out of a Siloed Sales Culture," last modified July 24, 2012, https://www.executiveboard.com/blogs/breaking-out-of-a-siloed-sales -culture/.
4. MHI Research Institute, "The Pursuit of World Class Performance," last modified October 13, 2014, https://www.millerheiman.com/getattachment/Knowledge _Center/Knowledge_Center_Articles/Sales_Performance_Research/2014-Miller -Heiman-Sales-Best-Practices-Study-Exec/2014-SBPS-ExecutiveSummary_MHI -Research-Institute.pdf.aspx/.
5. Tamara Schenk, "Conscious Collaboration—A Behavior of World Class Sales Per- formers," last modified July 21, 2014, https://www.millerheiman.com/blog/Miller -Heiman-Blog/July-2014/Conscious-Collaboration—A-Behavior-Of-World-Class/.
6. Alex Osborn, *How to Think Up* (New York: McGraw-Hill, 1942).
7. D. W. Taylor, P. C. Berry, and C. H. Block, "Does Group Participation Using Brainstorming Facilitate or Inhibit Creative Thinking?," *Administrative Science Quarterly* 6 (1958): 22–47.
8. Jonah Lehrer, "Groupthink: The Brainstorming Myth," last modified January 30, 2012, http://www.newyorker.com/magazine/2012/01/30/groupthink.
9. Charlan Nemeth, Bernard Personnaz, Marie Personnaz, and Jack Goncalo, "The Liberating Role of Conflict in Group Creativity: A Study in Two Countries," *Euro- pean Journal of Social Psychology* 34 (2004): 365–374. Available at http://char lannemeth.com/files/NPPGLiberatingRoleUSFR.pdf, last accessed June 14, 2015.

Chapter 4: Spinning Up a Solutions Web

1. Ed Catmull, Amy Wallace, *Creativity, Inc.: Overcoming the Unseen Forces That Stand in the Way of True Inspiration* (New York: Random House, 2014).
2. Morten Hansen, *Collaboration: How Great Leaders Avoid the Traps, Build Common Ground, and Reap Big Results* (Boston: Harvard Business Review Press, 2009).
3. Rich Karlgaard and Michael Malone, *Team Genius: The New Science of High Per- forming Organizations* (New York: HarperBusiness, 2015).
4. Cass Sunstein and Reid Hastie, *Wiser: Getting Beyond Groupthink to Make Groups Smarter* (Boston: Harvard Business Review Press, 2014).
5. Tom Kelley and David Kelley, *Creative Confidence: Unleashing the Creative Poten- tial in Us All* (New York: Crown Business, 2013).
6. David Burkus, *The Myths of Creativity: The Truth About How Innovative Companies and People Generate Great Ideas.* (San Francisco: Jossey Bass Wiley, 2013). eBook edition.
7. Lisa Gundry and Laurie LaMantia, *Breakthrough Teams for Breakneck Times: Unlocking the Genius of Creative Collaboration* (Chicago: Dearborn Trade Publish- ing, 2001).
8. Robert Hargrove, *Mastering the Art of Creative Collaboration* (New York: McGraw- Hill, 1997).

Chapter 5: Chance Favors the Prepared Mind

1. Lisa Gundry and Laurie LaMantia, *Breakthrough Teams for Breakneck Times: Unlocking the Genius of Creative Collaboration* (Chicago: Dearborn Trade Publishing, 2001).
2. Ibid.
3. Keith Sawyer, *Explaining Creativity: The Science of Human Innovation*, 2nd Edition (New York: Oxford University Press, 2012). eBook edition.
4. Mark Donnolo, *The Innovative Sale: Unleash Your Creativity for Better Customer Solutions and Extraordinary Results* (New York: Amacom, 2014).
5. Patricia D. Stokes, *Creativity from Constraints: The Psychology of Breakthrough* (New York: Springer, 2005).
6. David Burkus, *The Myths of Creativity: The Truth About How Innovative Companies and People Generate Great Ideas* (San Francisco: Jossey Bass Wiley, 2013). eBook edition.

Chapter 6: Making Meetings Magic

1. Quoted by Leigh Thompson, *Creative Conspiracy: The New Rules of Breakthrough Collaboration* (Boston: Harvard Business Review Press, 2013).
2. Quoted by Robert Hargrove, *Mastering the Art of Creative Collaboration* (New York: McGraw-Hill, 1997).
3. Leigh Thompson, *Creative Conspiracy: The New Rules of Breakthrough Collaboration* (Boston: Harvard Business Review Press, 2013).
4. Ibid.
5. Michael Wilkinson, *The Secrets of Facilitation: The S.M.A.R.T. Guide to Getting Results with Groups* (San Francisco: Jossey-Bass, 2004).
6. Dave Roach, Kim Troboy, and L. F. Cochran, "The Effects of Humor and Goal Setting on Individual Brainstorming Performance," *Journal of American Academy of Business* 9 (2006): 2.
7. Wilkinson, *The Secrets of Facilitation*.
8. Cass Sunstein and Reid Hastie, *Wiser: Getting Beyond Groupthink to Make Groups Smarter* (Boston: Harvard Business Review Press, 2014).
9. These six categories were developed during my consulting work as applicable to the sales process for most B2B companies. In April 2015, I surveyed twenty sales leaders who confirmed that these categories represent the most common causes of a sales challenge.
10. Thompson, *Creative Conspiracy*.
11. Keith Sawyer, *Group Genius: The Creative Power of Collaboration*, 2nd ed. (New York: Basic Books, 2008).
12. Alex Osborn, *Applied Imagination: Principles and Procedures of Creative Thinking* (New York: Scribner, 1953).
13. Peter Schwartz, *The Art of the Long View: Planning for the Future in an Uncertain World* (New York: Currency Doubleday, 1996).
14. Drew Boyd and Jacob Goldenberg, *Inside the Box: A Proven System of Creativity for Breakthrough Results* (New York: Simon & Schuster, 2014).
15. Wilkinson, *The Secrets of Facilitation*.

Notes

Chapter 7: Cleaning Up After the 'Storm

1. The W. Edwards Deming Institute, "The PDSA Cycle," accessed January 14, 2015, https://www.deming.org/theman/theories/pdsacycle.

Chapter 8: The Hacker, the Chef, and the Artist

1. The Edison Group, "The Social Habit," last modified December 3, 2014, http://www.edisonresearch.com/wp-content/uploads/2014/07/the-social-habit-2014.pdf.
2. Koka Sexton, "7 Real World Social Selling Examples to Inspire You," last modified November 6, 2014, http://sales.linkedin.com/blog/7-real-world-social-selling -examples-to-inspire-you/.
3. Emma Snider, "The Sales Professional's Go-To Guide to Social Selling," last modified May 18, 2015, http://blog.hubspot.com/sales/sales-professionals-guide-to-social -selling.
4. Andy Hertzfeld recalling Alan Kay's talk at Creative Think seminar, July 20, 1982, accessed June 6, 2015, http://www.folklore.org/StoryView.py?project=Macintosh& story=Creative_Think.txt.

Chapter 9: With a Little Help from Your Friends

1. This is the definition of "champion" (as in to champion one's cause); http://www .businessdictionary.com/definition/champion.html.
2. Karl Schmidt, Brent Adamson, and Anna Bird, "Making the Consensus Sale," last modified March 1, 2015, https://hbr.org/2015/03/making-the-consensus-sale.
3. Rizan Flenner, "How to Identify a Champion," last modified January 21, 2015, https://now.iseeit.com/how-to-identify-a-meddic-champion/.
4. Paul Weinstein, "To Close a Deal, Find a Champion," last modified November 5, 2014, https://hbr.org/2014/09/to-close-a-deal-find-a-champion/.
5. Schmidt, Adamson, and Bird, "Making the Consensus Sale."
6. Mark Suster, "The One Key Person That Will Help You Improve Your Sales," last modified January 17, 2014, http://www.bothsidesofthetable.com/2013/06/30/the -one-key-person-that-will-help-you-improve-sales/.
7. Quoted by Christopher Vogeler, *The Writer's Journey: Mythic Structure for Writers,* 3d ed. (Studio City, CA: Michael Wiese Productions, 2007).
8. Stephanie Yang, "The Most Powerful Person in Finance at Every Age," last modified July 3, 2014, http://www.businessinsider.com/most-powerful-people-in-finance -2014-6?op=1.
9. Suster, "The One Key Person That Will Help You Improve Your Sales."

Chapter 10: Innovation at the Relationship Exchange

1. Ieva Martinaityte and Claudia Sacramento, "When Creativity Enhances Sales Effectiveness: The Moderating Role of Leader–Member Exchange," *Journal of Organizational Behavior* 34 no. 7 (October 2013): 974–994.
2. Henry Chesbrough, executive director of the Open Center for Innovation at UC Berkeley in a lecture given at Yahoo! in 2004.

3. Susan DelVecchio, "The Quality of Salesperson-Manager Relationship: The Effect of Latitude, Loyalty and Competence," *Journal of Personal Selling and Sales Management* 18 no. 1 (1998): 31–47.
4. Richard Dienesch, "An Empirical Investigation of the Relationship Between Quality of Leader-Member Exchange and Subordinate Performance and Satisfaction," PhD dissertation, Georgia Institute of Technology (1987).
5. Judith Volmer, Daniel Spurk, and Cornelia Niessen, "Leader-Member Exchange (LMX), Job Autonomy, and Creative Work Involvement," *The Leadership Quarterly* 23 (2012): 456–465.
6. John Maslyn and Mary Uhl-Bien, "Leader-Member Exchange and Its Dimensions: Effects of Self-Effort and Other's Effort on Relationship Quality," *Journal of Applied Psychology* 86 no. 4 (2001): 697–708.
7. Susanne G. Scott and Reginald A. Bruce, "Determinants of Innovative Behavior: A Path Model of Individual Innovation in the Workplace," *The Academy of Management Journal* 37 no. 3 (1994): 580–607.

Conclusion: Why Everyone Should Weather a 'Storm

1. Jessica Shambora, "Define Reality and Give Hope," last modified May 12, 2009, http://fortune.com/2009/05/12/amex-ceo-ken-chenault-define-reality-and-give-hope/.
2. Brian Uzzi and Jarrett Spiro, "Collaboration and Creativity: The Small World Problem," *American Journal of Sociology* 111 no. 2 (September 2005).

Recommended Reads

The following nine books serve as a complement to *Dealstorming*. They offer useful insights on how to lead, facilitate, and innovate your way to victory.

Challenger Sale: Taking Control of the Customer Conversation by Matt Dixon and Brent Adamson

This book is based on groundbreaking research by the Corporate Executive Board, which reveals that the top-performing B2B salespeople challenge their customers, creating constructive tension and pressing them to change the way they do business. This runs counter to the long-standing relationship-selling philosophy that emphasizes hustle, nurturing, and conforming to the buyer's journey.

The Challenger Customer by Brent Adamson, Matthew Dixon, Pat Spenner, and Nick Toman

This followup to *Challenger Sale* expands on the rising complexity that today's B2B seller faces, adding buyer-team dysfunction to the mix. The key to success, they write, is to find mobilizers inside prospect companies that can marshal resources, support, and action to drive the sale. The book offers excellent tools for sellers to use in preparing a mobilizer to be an effective advocate of their solutions.

The Innovative Sale: Unleash Your Creativity for Better Customer Solutions by Mark Donnolo

In a challenging sales situation, it's important to find the balance between the creative right brain and process-oriented left brain approaches. Donnolo leverages his success in both the creative arts and enterprise sales to offer several ways to approach problem solving using innovative thinking. His sections on challenging assumptions and then reframing the problem are especially helpful, as these practices will only sharpen your focus on the real issues with your prospective sale.

Group Genius: The Creative Power of Collaboration by Keith Sawyer

By studying how jazz ensembles, improv comedy groups, and theatrical groups collectively produce stellar performances, Sawyer realized that all creative breakthroughs come from teams. He offers ways to cultivate your own creative tendency in the context of your group performance. Key takeaways include how to contribute to collaborative group dynamics and how to build on others' ideas.

Wiser: Getting Beyond Groupthink to Make Groups Smarter by Cass Sunstein and Reid Hastie

These experts on collaborative meetings understand why groups can amplify bad thinking as much as produce innovative ideas. This book explains how "happy talk" is the enemy of effective meetings, and how to get everyone in the room to be candid and "reveal what they know." Their examples range from government crisis resolution to corporate product development.

The Secrets of Facilitation: The S.M.A.R.T. Guide to Getting Results with Groups by Michael Wilkinson

This textbook is based on decades of facilitation experience in every industry. Wilkinson offers step-by-step methods for organizing and facilitating project groups that often reach consensus, which is the key to successful execution of ideas that come from collaborative meetings. This is a must read for any dedicated facilitation resource, as it dives deeply into dealing with dysfunction, keeping diverse groups on track and in the same conversation, and preserving relationships even when meetings don't turn out as planned.

Creativity, Inc.: Overcoming the Unseen Forces That Stand in the Way of Innovation by Ed Catmull and Amy Wallace

This book is part memoir and part management tome, and highly entertaining. Pixar's Ed Catmull ruminates about the creative, technical, and human challenges that his company faced over its history. Starting with *Toy Story*, his collaborative SWAT team (the Brain Trust) unleashed innovation by reducing the barriers to candor—which he believes is the secret to leadership success.

Tell to Win: Connect, Persuade and Triumph with the Hidden Power of Story by Peter Guber

This will build on your ability to win at the convince level of the sale. During his deal-making career, Guber demonstrated the power of the story device in moving people to value his ideas and respond to his calls for action. The book shares examples of how entrepreneurs, politicians, and business professionals have mastered the "art of the tell."

Multipliers: How the Best Leaders Make Everyone Smarter by Liz Wiseman and Greg McKeown

There are two types of managers: the diminisher and the multiplier. The former considers himself the brain and his team the hands. The latter wants to hire and mentor people whom she will someday work for. This book offers ways to become a multiplier manager who stretches her team members to expand their abilities and ambitions. This is key to leading a sales team today, where multiplying the competency of your people is the only way to scale your long-term success.

Index

Index

LaMantia, Laurie, 76
Lane Bryant, 188
Lasseter, John, 29–30, 57–59
Lawrence, Nina, 201
Leader-member exchange. *See* LMX
Lehman Brothers, 170
LG Architects, 167–68
Likeability Factor, The (Sanders), 196
Limited, The, 187–88
Lincoln, Abraham, 82
LinkedIn
    contact level of the sale, 32–33
    influence map in deal brief,
      86–87
    market penetration, 25, 64
    networking or referrals, 159,
      161–62, 195–96
Linkner, Josh, 162–63
Livesay, John, 128–29, 179–84, 191,
    200–201, 214
LMX, 201–17
Lone genius myth, 30–31, 46–49, 146
LoPresti, Anthony, 166–67
Lucent, 76

McCarthy, Patrick, 181
McSally, Mike, 46
Malone, Michael, 67
Manic Miner (video game), 27
Marciano, Paul, 180–84
Marcus, Stanley, Jr., 169, 170, 210–11
Martinaityte, Ieva, 201
Mastering the Art of Collaboration
    (Hargrove), 78
Mastering the Complex Sale
    (Thull), 26
Meeting roles, 69–76
    information master, 69, 74–75
    problem owner, 69–70
    resources, 69, 69*n*, 71–74
    sponsor, 69–71

Meeting team formation, 60–80
    confirming participation, 78–80
    organize step, 7, 68–80
    Pixar's *Toy Story* case, 57–59
    qualify step, 7, 60–68
    recruiting candidates, 76–78
    roles in meeting. *See* Roles in
      meeting
    size of team, 68–69
Microsoft, 73
Miklusak, Neil, 25, 64
Miller Heiman Research Institute,
    50–51
Miller Heiman Strategic Selling, 9, 208
Milligan, Jay, 174
Miltenberger, Bill, 155–56
Monster, 39, 40, 43
Moore's Law, 169
Moran, Gerry, 159
Morphology of the Folktale (Propp), 191
Motley Fool, 25
Motorola, 97
Murnighan, Keith, 99
Myths of Creativity, The (Burkus),
    47, 48

Napoleon Bonaparte, 219
NB+C, 196–98
Neiman Marcus, 169, 210–11
Nelson, Mark, 51, 104, 161
Nemeth, Charlan, 53
No influence and no authority
    (NINAs), 189–90
Novell, 24, 151

Office, The (TV show), 105
Opportunity Village, 167–68
Oracle, 18, 25, 33, 195
Oracle Cloud, 74, 129, 214, 220
Organize step, 7, 68–80
    confirming participation, 78–80

Williams, Jessica, 50

Wiser: Getting Beyond Groupthink to Make Groups Smarter (Sunstein and Hastie), 71, 98, 234

Woodward, Stan, 1–2, 3, 11, 208–9, 218

World of Warcraft (video game), 16

Wozniak, Steve, 47

Wright, Frank Lloyd, 90, 141

Yahoo!, 3–6, 77. *See also* ValueLab

Yale University, 52